The Negotiation Jungle

The Negotiation Jungle

400+ Tricks and Tactics to Help You Survive

Brendan Anglin & Cristina Manso

A Green Cat Book

Madrid

2015

A Green Cat Book

Publishing History

Green Cat Editorial paperback edition 2015

Published by Green Cat Editorial

Madrid, Madrid

Copyright © 2015 Brendan Anglin

The moral right of the author has been asserted

ISBN 9788494419409

To Daniel, Ana and Eric
who always get what they want.

And to Trin,
thanks for the red scissors.

Contents

"Information is a negotiator's greatest weapon"

- *Victor Kiam*

First Steps in the Jungle

We all negotiate, all the time, whether we are aware of it or not. From work – salaries with bosses, contracts with clients, window seats with coworkers – to personal – restaurant choices with friends, t.v. remote controls with partners, and everything with children. Improving our ability to negotiate (not lie or cheat or attack) will therefore mean greater returns for us, and hopefully for our counterparts too. This can only mean a general improvement in our lives as a whole.

This book, therefore, aims to arm you with greater knowledge about the different people you will encounter in a negotiation context, and the tactics they, and you, may use. By doing so this book will help you achieve better outcomes and make your negotiations more successful.

Let's start our adventure into the Jungle by answering the following two questions. **First**: Why call this book *The Negotiation Jungle*? **and second:** Why should *you* read this book?

Let's begin answering the first question by asking another – what images and feelings does the word "jungle" conjure up in the minds of most people?

12 The Negotiation Jungle

Some people see the jungle as a place where they can die from malaria, be eaten by some wild animal, be sucked into a smothering death in a stretch of quick sand or drowned in a swamp, they could be poisoned by some spider that doesn't shave it's legs and has more eyes than an old potatoe, die from a festering cut, fall down a vine covered ravine, be squeezed to death by an enormous snake....... I think you've got the picture.

At the same time many other people love the freedom that jungles represent - no rules but great opportunities, as if each jungle had an ancient temple at it's centre with a ruby the size of an ostrich egg, or a creature yet to be discovered. Adventurers, full of self confidence and ready for any challenge, see the jungle as a place where they can feel truly alive.

In reality both images of the jungle are true – it can be a dangerous place for the unwary and the unprepared, but it can also be a world full of excitement and great opportunities.

Negotiations can be the same, though thankfully for most of us they are rarely lethal. For most of us negotiating is part of our daily business - from building a motorway across the desert to purchasing toilet paper for the company, or for personal reasons - to get a salary raise, or buy a new car for example. These negotiations generally provide the opportunity to improve our lives, sometimes dramatically, but only if they go well   As a result negotiations can cause spikes in our stress levels and these spikes can cause one of the three animal reactions that stress produced in our very distant ancestors who actually lived in a jungle – fight, flee or freeze.

None of these reactions are necessarily wrong. The problem however is not fighting, fleeing or freezing. The problem is reacting with instincts honed milennia ago in one jungle when you are faced with potential threats or stressful situations in another "jungle".

Greater knowledge of the negotiation "jungle" can help us decide which action (or reaction) to take – fight, flight, freeze or friend. Sometimes you do have to fight –say 'No', dig in and argue your position, go on the attack, or ask for more. Sometimes you should freeze – stop, be careful, listen, wait, take stock. Sometimes you should flee – give in, give away, agree, change your expectations. Just like in the jungle however there are times when none of the three typical reactions to stress are a good idea. Intsead you should just calm down and then build trust and find to find a mutual solution to the problem at hand.

The Jungle was chosen as a metaphor precisely for all the reasons mentioned so far; it has a variety of animals, which in our case represent the myriad of negotiating personalities you may meet on your negotiation odyssey; it has danger, which represents the possibility of you losing a deal, your raise, or your job; it has that ancient temple at its heart which represents the great gains that can be achieved if you negotiate correctly; and it has freedom which refers to the lack of rules of behaviour in most negotiations – creating both opportunities and threats.

Just like a real jungle you can conquer the negotiation "jungle" through planning and preparation: you can learn what might bite you; what plants you can eat; where to put your hammock. Likewise in a negotiation you can prepare and learn what you should ask for; what is the standard policy in a specific industry; and what are the fees charged for certain services, for example.

In both the real jungle and the negotiation jungle it also means accepting the fact that despite all your preparation there is very little you can do if an elephant sits on you. Sometimes you have to live with the fact that you are not going to get what you want and that you have to put this particular negotiation down to a learning experience. Then you get up, dust yourself off and get ready for the next part of your life.

Question 2: Why should you read this book?

Let's return to a concept introduced in the previous section: the idea of negotiating creating stress in many people, (from a slight racing of your pulse to a complete panic attack). The *IDEA* of negotiating creates stress in many people.

This book aims at reducing those feelings of stress, and any worries you may have about your ability to cope, by making you more prepared for what is out there, so you will not only survive but thrive. Knowing the pitfalls, knowing the traps, knowing the poisons, knowing the personalities, the dangerous ones, the gentle ones, all of this knowledge and information makes it more likely that you will survive your own particular negotiation jungle.

A word of warning however. This book will not turn you into a negotiation superhero. That elephant can still sit on you and squash you. However if you take on board the advice, read the personality types and the 400+ tricks & tactics herein you will negotiate consistently better and be more successful, both personally and profesionally.

16 The Negotiation Jungle

The Negotiation Jungle©

While it is true that there are a myriad of personalities in the world, there are only a limited number of responses to conflict. Typically these are divided into five: conceder, competitive, avoider, compromiser and collaborator (principled). They range from putting one's own interests first and not caring about the other side (competitive), to caring about the other's interests and not being assertive about one's own (conceder) through being both assertive and thinking of the other side's interests (collaborator).

In most of the literature on negotiations these five (or sometimes less) approaches to conflict are then stretched to refer to the negotiating styles that exist in the world. It has been our experience that five approaches to conflict are not sufficient to describe the variety of negotiating styles that exist in the real world.

For example, in the traditional division of negotiation styles both a bully that attacks you and insults you in an effort to get what they want, and a charmer that lies to you and uses schmooze and seduction to achieve their goals are both grouped under the same label of 'competitive negotiator'. Under that label you will also find grouped someone who uses cold numbers and statistics to blind you, rubbing shoulders with people who use emotion and bluster. Adopting the same strategy to deal with all of these negotiating styles would clearly not be effective.

Working instead within the metaphor of the jungle we have identified sixteen different "animal" negotiating styles to make it easier for you to quickly label behaviours in a negotiation setting and rapidly build defences and appropriate responses.

We have chosen Zoomorphism (giving animals human characteristics) as the mnemonic device to help you understand and recall the different negotiation styles. We have done this because we feel that using the shorthand of saying 'I would watch this person because he is a chimpanzee' or 'she is a tiger, so be careful' makes it easier to identify families of tactics that may be used against you, and also aids communication in a team when analysing your counterparts on the other side of the table.

In each of the animals you will find references to some of the 400+ tricks and tactics found in the second half of the book. These will either be in bold in the text or listed in the section of 'Common Tricks and Tactics of a *Chimpanzee*. You can look these up to get a better idea of the kind of strategies adopted by each negotiating style.

You will notice that even though this book is called the Negotiation Jungle some of the animals below are not specifically found in a Jungle (Ostriches, eagles, owls, vultures, rhinos, porcupines, for example). In the case of these animals we ask your forgiveness. We felt that calling the book 'How to Survive the Negotiation Jungle, Forest and Savannah' was unnecessarily complicating things.

Please read on and see if you can identify yourself or anyone you know.

The Negotiating Circle and the Jungle

As already mentioned, we have identified sixteen negotiating styles that correspond in this book to different animals. We have placed these on a Negotiating Circle which takes in the five main elements running through all negotiations.

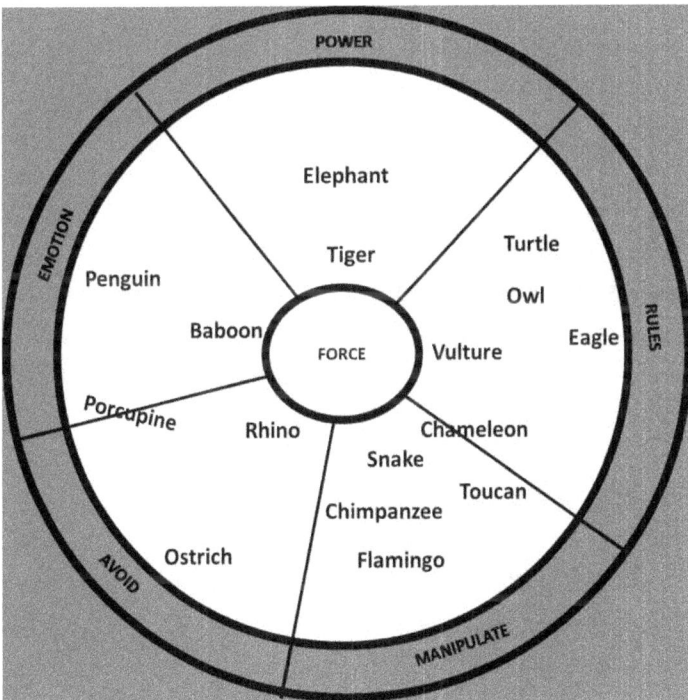

Power

The ones closer to the centre are those who are happier with conflict, force and agression and care less for the other side than their own needs. Those who are closer to the edge are less inclined to look for conflict, and avoid using force and agression.

In the Power section belong the groups that essentially view a negotiation as a power play, and if you have more power, then you get what you want. They spend more time building and searching for power than thinking about the specific mechanics of the negotiation or creative solutions.

Manipulate

In the Manipulate section there are those that believe primarily in lies, deception and wordplay to get what they want, regardless of who actually has the power. Negotiators in this group may range from the softer uses of manipulation (where you are actually happy to oblige them) to full blown dirty tricks, cheating and deceit which lie closer to the centre.

Rules

In the rules section are those people who believe in either using rules and precedents to batter the other side into submission, or to use rules and precedents to create a fair, unemotional solution to the negotiation problem.

Emotion

The Emotion group believes that emotions and people are the key to negotiations. In the case of Penguins that means 'if I am nice to them and give them everything they want then they will like me and they will be nice to me.' In the case of a baboon, close to the centre, it means using emotion as a weapon. There are other styles, like the Flamingo, that also use emotion but only as one of their many tools of manipulation.

Avoid

The last section, the avoiding group, does not like to negotiate and expresses their stance by either not giving in on anything, or avoiding negotiations completely, even if that means hurting themselves.

Of course if you are dealing with a pragmatic competitive negotiator you may find that they switch from one style to another to suit the demands of the negotiation, and the weaknesses of their counterparts. They may not have a preferred 'animal' style which they slip into. Rather they have the attitude of using whatever works in the moment as long as they get what they want.

You may also find that depending on the circumstances even people who are not opportunistic negotiators also change their negotiating style, though they may do so without any conscious thought. For example, a Tiger, when they find themselves with no power, turns into a Penguin or a Flamingo more often than you might expect.

In the next part of the book we are going to look at these sixteen animals in more detail, their common characteristics, how to deal with them, and the tricks and tactics they generally use or like to use.

1. Penguins

Common Characteristics

You may ask yourself, "What the hell are penguins doing in the jungle?"

Exactly.

They shouldn't be there. Dressed up in their little tuxedos they would be fine at some formal dinner party in an igloo. They look cuddly and if you're a seal they make a great kebab. They swim extremely well and the male of the species can sit on an egg all winter without doing anything else. Laudable, especially from the egg's point of view.

In the jungle, however, they are useless. Their black and white pattern serves as zero camouflage, unless they are standing in front of a zebra. Waddling will never make it as an Olympic sport and certainly makes it difficult to escape a cheetah coming at them at 70 mph. Those flappy wings are good for making them look like they are panicking but couldn't fend off a sausage. Penguins have not been designed by nature to survive in the jungle.

Some people in a negotiation are like penguins in the jungle. They are the worst possible negotiators. They only survive if they find a jungle full of other penguins i.e. not actually a jungle.

The world is full of Penguin negotiators. They sacrifice their own interests and needs to save the relationship with the other person. They give in whenever there is a negotiation. They may turn into an ostrich or porcupine in future (avoiding negotiations completely) or eventually get fed up and start to use aggressive tactics of their own so in the long term you may find that your penguin has transformed into altogether another animal (Rhino, Tiger, Snake?).

In the short term however the Penguin becomes mincemeat for competitive negotiators.

The Good News (if you are a Penguin negotiator) is that people, unlike Penguins, can change. We are not condemned to waddle our way to a grisly end in the jungle. By reading the tricks in the following pages and arming yourself with the knowledge of how to deal with other negotiators, taking a course on assertiveness and talking to someone about the anxiety that the thought of a negotiation creates in you, it is possible to leave your flightless, plush toy days behind you and become an Eagle negotiator.

How to deal with a Penguin Negotiator

If you are a competitive negotiator and the following conditions apply then you will probably take advantage of the Penguin's softness and vulnerability.

If it's A) a short term negotiation, B) you will never see them again and C) they have authority to take a decision. In these circumstances it becomes a sad case of Penguin Pie time.

However if they have no authority to take a decision then it can be very frustrating for all concerned as they give away a lot in the negotiation, reach a bad deal for their own side and then no-one on their side will sign off on it. They are stressed and flustered by the negotiation process itself and you do not get what you want at the end.

If this is going to be a long term negotiation then you should try and build them up, praise them and make them feel good about themselves and their ideas. This way they will make concessions to you simply because they are so happy at being treated well. If they have no authority and you treat them well you will find that they talk with their superiors for you and defend your position.

If you have to deal with them regularly then be careful of taking advantage of them early on because you may find that when they realise what has happened they start to get overly aggressive later to compensate for their failure early on and their lack of negotiating skill.

Common Tricks & Tactics of a Penguin

Zero. Unless, perhaps they are along the lines of a puppy dog that rolls over so you can scratch it's stomach.

2. Chimpanzee

Common Characteristics

Chimpanzees are intelligent, dextrous and they have big gummy grins. They can adapt to different situations and do not look very threatening. Yeah right. Do not trust the gingival grin. In the wild these guys are far from friendly. Sure they eat nuts and fruit – but they also eat meat. They are very strong, work well in a group and can hunt down monkeys and enemy chimpanzees like army special forces. If they spot a Penguin walking into their Jungle you can see their eyes literally lighting up.

Chimpanzees are very clever creatures, and know the negotiating game very well. They are actors that feel at home with double talk. They use timing and false promises and false trails. They typically use red herrings, bogus issues that you spend time negotiating on so they can appear to concede later on these issues in return for movement from you on another area. They also use false promises to give the appearance that they are helping you with no intention of delivering on those promises. They invent false deadlines that they push you up against.

They regularly say that they have no money, that their pockets are empty, that they are very interested in your offer but just do not have the money to pay for it at present, unless the price was reduced somewhat. Every time they make a concession they make it out to be a big deal and a major sacrifice on their part. Every time you ask for something they flinch to indicate that it will be very difficult for them to move on this issue.

When you try to get them to sign a contract they tell you they have no authority. And finally when you have reached the stage where you are going to sign the contract and you are excited about doing so they hesitate and add in extra points that were never agreed before.

How to deal with a Chimpanzee Negotiator

When dealing with them you have to be very patient. Do not be forced up against their deadlines, the only deadlines you should worry about are your own. Smile to yourself when they flinch. If you have done your homework correctly then you should know that there is nothing unreasonable about your demands.

Do not get defensive with them as you will only stop thinking clearly and make mistakes. Instead you should view this as a game, just like they do, and try to mentally register every trick they are using and congratulate yourself for having noticed them.

Before negotiating too hard on any particular subject you should test to be sure that it is a real issue and not one invented to later concede. To avoid the fact that they will definitely pad their figures you should ask them to justify how they have arrived at those amounts. Do not get excited about any promises they make until they are in the contract and you will also have to plan to have clauses in the contract specifically stating what will happen if the contract is not implemented correctly (lifeboat clause). See **Test Assumptions** in the Tricks & Tactics part of this book**.**

Do not make any concessions at the end to simply close the deal if they start hesitating. You may feel that you are only conceding 5% but when you are talking about a deal worth millions that could well be your bonus gone up in smoke just because they hesitated (see **Quivering Quill**)

Common Tricks & Tactics of a Chimpanzee

All of the following tricks and tactics are in the second part of this book, listed alphabetically: *Anchoring, Adding and subtracting, Answering a question with a question, Bracketing, Brooklyn optician, Comparing, Conceal, Crocodile tears, Cry me a river (of gold), Culture C – Forgive me and let me keep on doing it, Decoy, Disinterest, Distract and sign, Empty pockets,*

Empty promises, False deadlines, False memories, Financial year, Flinch and wince, Haggle with a hobgoblin, "I'm afraid my boss won't agree", Just a little servant, Launching a tangent, Legalise Cocaine!, Major Sacrifice, Padding;, Paper Crown, Quivering quill, Rags, Red herring, Reluctant seller/ buyer, Straw man, The model on sale is sold out but we have this other one...., Widows and orphans, Your competition......, Cherry picking, "Appeal to their better nature", 9/10s of the law.

3. Elephants

Common Characteristics

Elephants are big, *very* big, and they know they are.

Elephant negotiators believe that size matters, and very often it does, but not always (you might be a mouse that scares the hell out of them). Because they are big they believe that they are always right and that they have the power to dictate the terms in a negotiation. If you are a smaller company they will tell you that you should reduce your prices or terms with them so that you can become famous and make money somewhere else in future. They will expect you to follow set procedures that they have in place and you may also expect serious delays in getting paid.

"Hey, you should be happy to have our business, don't expect to be paid as well!"

Their offices are often huge and sumptuously decorated. They may arrive in a flashy car and dressed expensively. Their conversation may be peppered with name dropping. When you are there they may even deal with other people and answer other calls to make you feel inconsequential.

They have more money, more people and more resources than you and if they use hospitality it will not be so much about schmoozing you as "shock and awing" you.

How to deal with an Elephant Negotiator

Before you enter a negotiation with an Elephant you should seriously consider whether it is worth doing business with them. Is this simply an ego thing? Do you want to have the biggest client on the block? If this is the case then you should be careful about doing business with a behemoth that will make no money for you, tie up a lot of your resources, and potentially destroy your cash flow.

If you do decide that it is worthwhile doing business with them then you should be sure to add a plus to your prices to compensate you for late payment. You should emphasise your differences with your competitors to avoid competing with other suppliers on price. Do not be intimidated by large offices or fancy cars.

Expect to be left waiting for long periods of time so be sure to bring a good book/magazine or work on your laptop. You may also have to sit patiently during the negotiations while they deal with other people or other calls. You will have to be patient and try not to be too sensitive. Getting angry here will not help your position as they are used to being in power and react badly to being provoked, to the extent that they may not agree to a deal that would be good for both of you.

If your preferred negotiating style happens to be a Flamingo Negotiator then you can flatter them or create extra issues for them that they can demolish so they feel like they are winning and that they are important. (See **Ego trap**)

Common Tricks & Tactics of an Elephant

All of the following tricks and tactics are in the second part of this book, listed alphabetically: *"Sorry, you were saying...., Status, Big Car, Big office, Big reputation, Big title, Big dresser,: COTS, Deep pockets, Fame, Keeping you waiting, Money in the bank.*

4. Flamingo

Common Characteristics

Beautiful, pink, poised on one leg. Working so well as part of a flock a thousand wide. Their reflection shimmering on the surface of a lake in Africa. How could a Flamingo possibly be considered dangerous?

Flamingo Negotiators are excellent at flattery and making you feel good so they can take advantage of you. This type of negotiator will try to develop a friendship with you so that you will then make concessions. They may do this by giving gifts, using excessive hospitality and inventing points they have in common with you.

They abuse the concept of reciprocity. Most of the time what you must give back has real value and what you have received has very little.   That will not stop them from saying things like 'I scratch your back, you scratch mine' or 'one good turn deserves another'.

They will also try to make you feel sorry for them by telling you how hard you are making their side suffer and they will give you the impression that you will feel like a much better person if you make concessions. A variation of this will be to talk about how they are having a hard time with their own boss and that you should try and put yourself in their shoes. They may say that if you help them this time then they will help you next time (something which never happens).

They will tell you how great you are and pretend to be very innocent and inexperienced. They may use sex to persuade you, using beautiful women and handsome men to seduce you or simply to flatter and fluster you. No sex has to actually happen for this to be an effective tool. Some people try to impress or please the Flamingo in return, by making concessions they normally wouldn't make, or else they stop thinking clearly or are thinking so happily that they make concessions that would seem extremely generous if they were more calm and collected.

How to deal with a Flamingo Negotiator

It can be very difficult to deal with this style if you are not prepared. However if you go into the negotiation from the beginning with the idea that you must separate the people from the issue and not be influenced by your feelings for the person when it comes to the substantive issues on the table then you have at least started to prepare yourself. (See **Separate people**)

It is important to realise that we are human beings and our emotions are generally not separate from the logical part of our minds. We generally try to create a positive atmosphere with the other negotiator either for ourselves to make the negotiating process easier or for them to make it more likely that they will want to do business with us again[1]. It is easy to then overstep this positive feeling and make goodwill gestures in the form of concessions on tangible issues.

It should be established before the negotiation what kind of throwaway gestures can be made to create or maintain good feeling and rapport, and what are the substantive issues that are independent of a good working relationship. By having your objectives clear both as a negotiator and a company you can still use empathy without becoming a charity. You can still be entertained and take advantage of their hospitality without giving in on the issues being negotiated. (See **Preparation** and **Prioritise**.)

You have to constantly remind yourself that this is a negotiation and that no matter how good you are made to feel *during* the negotiation the truly important thing is that you feel good *after* the negotiation.

---

[1] Though there are negotiators who deliberately make the atmosphere as unpleasant as possible to either make you rush through the process or to avoid relaxing and making concessions like those listed above. See Tiger, Baboon, Snake.

Common Tricks & Tactics of a Flamingo

All of the following tricks and tactics are in the second part of this book, listed alphabetically: *Appeal to your heart, Big favour, little favour, Ego trap, Fake smile, Flattery, Friendship, Full stomach, Gifts, Golf, Halo effect, Honey trap, Hospitality, Humour, In-group-out-group, Kissing babies, Massaging a big ego, Mirroring and Pacing, My boss is a b*st*rd, Never Say No, Reciprocation, Relationship, Rub smooth, Sex, Smile a mile, We're all friends here...., "Go easy on me".*

5. Tiger

Common Characteristics

Power. Claws. Teeth. Man-eaters. Extremely dangerous.

The Tiger is the most typical of the competitive negotiators - they are generally bullies who threaten and attack you. They may say they are going to destroy your name and reputation. They may use blackmail. They may use threats of court, strikes, dismissals, walk outs or war. They will very often give you what is called the Russian front option: two bad options of which one is slightly less bad and they make you choose.

They can enter your personal space, intimidate you with their physical size if they are bigger or even push you. They may make personal attacks on your personality, age, clothes, your time keeping, and your organisation - anything that will make you feel bad. They may talk over you, interrupt you, shout you down. They look for weaknesses and try to exploit them and highlight them.

Sometimes they are simply pushing to see if they can get away with it and to see how you will react, and if they do not perceive weakness they will change tactics immediately. Other times they will simply continue, as this is their personality and they do not know any other way of acting.

When you think of Tiger Negotiators think of force, fear, aggression.

How to deal with a Tiger Negotiator

The first thing you have to do is mentally prepare yourself before you go in and to be clear about your goals, your walk away position, your alternatives and the fact that they can say or do whatever they want but you will not lose sight of those goals. (See **Separate People**)

You can either ignore their tactics and focus on the issues, or you can ask them to change their behaviour if they want to continue the negotiation. It may be necessary in some cases to call in a mediator to act as a go-between if the other side continues their personal attacks and aggressive behaviour. But the essential thing is not to make concessions to placate them. That way you are simply telling them their bullying tactics are working and they will continue to use them with you. As Heywood C. Broun aptly said "Appeasers believe that if you keep on throwing steaks to a tiger, the tiger will become a vegetarian".

What you must not do is respond in kind. If they are bullies these are tactics that work for them, and if you enter a battle of wills in an area that you normally don't work in, then there is a greater chance that you will lose. If you move the negotiation from the substantive issues into the highly charged and emotional personal arena then there is a greater chance that you will come out with a worse deal (or no deal). You may also find that if you use bullying tactics in return they will then suddenly play innocent and blame you for a break down in the negotiations (something which would imply that you have to make a concession to restart the negotiations).

Common Tricks & Tactics of a Tiger

All of the following tricks and tactics are in the second part of this book, listed alphabetically: *Bad publicity, Blackmail, Coercion, Fear, Force projection, "My friend Vincent...", Or else, Outnumbering, Overt intimidation, Personal Insults, Physical intimidation, Punish Power, Running down your product and your service, Russian front, "See you in court!", The long walk, Threaten, Ultimatum, War, What do you know?, You've got to be kidding me/ you can't be serious, Big Body, Good cop bad cop, Big head-ing, Take it or leave it.*

6. Snake

Common Characteristics

Rarely do people put Snakes in the category of 'honest', 'straightforward', 'trustworthy', 'fair'. As long as stories have been written snakes have been getting a bad rap. Amazonian tree frogs are more poisonous and snails have the same number of legs and arms, yet the Snake is the one that is considered dangerous, sneaky and impossible to trust. We will leave it up to someone else, somewhere else, to argue the case of the Snake, in this book the Snake represents all the negative stereotypes out there about them.

Snake negotiators have a natural tendency to try and undermine you and your side to their advantage. They use techniques such as divide and conquer, covert intimidation, spying and laying false information.

You would do well to make sure with these people, that the room you have been given for team meetings has not been bugged, or there is no speaker phone turned on that people outside can be listening to. The speakerphone may even be used when you are negotiating with a junior on their side and a manager comes in at a strategic moment to close a deal or offer support (after having been outside listening covertly to the entire meeting). If you speak a language other than the language that is being used in the negotiation they will have someone on their team who is there exclusively because they speak your language and is there to listen in on your supposedly impenetrable conversations.

When it comes to trying to pin a Snake down on a certain point they are suddenly missing information or the person with the relevant material can't be found.

While they will use language such as 'give it to me straight' or 'help me to understand' what they are in fact trying to do is gather as much intelligence about your position as possible without giving anything back. They will disguise themselves as Owl negotiators when it suits their purposes.

They will most certainly answer your questions with questions of their own. They may leave papers where you can find them about their position; these documents might be planted or even false. They may resort to bribery and they will certainly try to find the weakest member of your team to try and separate them and develop a fifth column. You may find that the local lawyer, interpreter or adviser you are using is in fact working for their side.

The covert intimidation techniques that they will use against you consist of tactics such as leaving the door behind you open so you feel uncomfortable that you are being listened to, only enough space for three on your side of the table even though your team consists of four, no water and the air conditioning turned off in a hot country, no breaks for food, lower chairs or seats that slope forward or have one leg shorter so you spend more time trying to stay on your seat than thinking about what they are saying.

The very obvious will have the sunlight in your eyes when you enter the room. The more effective will make sure that you have the sunlight in your eyes at the crucial bargaining phase when you are trying to think fast. They will also stretch out the negotiation so that you are physically tired and not thinking clearly. This may be especially true if it is in territory where they can take regular breaks and rest well while you suffer.

How to deal with a Snake Negotiator

The first thing is to accept that your body can betray you if you are not aware of it. People who are tired, hungry, under physical pressure and in discomfort do not think and negotiate as well as people who are. If you find that you are in this kind of situation then ask your counterparts to rectify the situation. It is always possible that they are thoughtless as opposed to crafty. If they invent excuses for continuing your discomfort then you have gained valuable information. You know that you are negotiating with a Snake and you should be on your guard.

If they put you in an uncomfortable, small, wonky chair then cite a bad back and ask to change it for theirs. If the door is open and protocol permits it then get up and close it yourself. If you are travelling somewhere else, especially another country, then give your body time to adjust to the new timetable, jetlag, food, temperature and air.

If you feel that your place of caucus, hotel or computer are compromised then use this time as an opportunity to gather information but be very careful about sharing your opinions or your own position with the rest of your team until you are in a place that is definitely secure. Do not trust any information that you are given until you have had time to check it. If you find that all your questions are being answered with questions then it is very normal to negotiate how many questions each side gets to ask.

Common Tricks & Tactics of a Snake

All of the following tricks and tactics are in the second part of this book, listed alphabetically: *Alcohol, Bribery, Covert Intimidation, Deliberate error, Divide and conquer, Double agent, Fatigue, Hunger, Leaking, Light in your eyes, Listening devices, Location, Missing person manoeuvre, No air con and no water, Open door, Planted information, Priming, Props, Skimmers, Small chairs and tall tables, Spies, Squashed at a table, Tech smart, Wolf in sheep's clothing.*

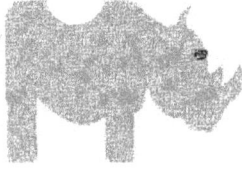

7. Rhino

Common Characteristics

They look slow and ponderous, don't they? Yet when they pick up speed they are the tanks of the natural world, ploughing through everything in a straight line. They are not particularly famous for their flexibility and acrobatics. Neither are Rhino negotiators.

Rhinos are stubborn. They are in the avoiding group of negotiators but they use their stubbornness as a deliberate hard tactic to avoid bargaining and making concessions, as opposed to trying to avoid the negotiation itself.

They very often quote company policy and their national culture as a reason for not changing their position. They use commitment ploys such as making public declarations and statements before the negotiation starts properly so it is difficult for them to change afterwards.

They come forward with standard terms, minimum orders and non-negotiable items from the word go and stick to them like barnacles to a boat. They will use phrases such as 'we've never done that before' and the much stronger 'take it or leave it'. They may continue to repeat their position *ad nauseam* or the alternative -complete silence - until you break and make a concession.

They act independently and implement things before they have been fully agreed with the other side so that they become *fait accompli* and are harder to change. The other side accepts this or risks scuppering the whole deal. They may even do this after the negotiation has been officially agreed - working on the premise that it is easier to say sorry than ask permission.

How to deal with a Rhino Negotiator

There is no point in taking a rhino head on as they will simply become more entrenched in their position. Instead of using the question 'why' (because the word 'why' can sometimes come across as accusatory) it is better to use phrases such 'what makes you feel like that?' or 'how was the company policy put together?' or 'how did you arrive at that position?

There are very few positions that cannot be negotiated. While it is very common for people to use policy and culture as reasons for not changing these are generally excuses as opposed to statements of truth. Even in a shop many assistants have some discretion to lower the ticket price on goods. Try it. You can lose nothing and you might gain 10% off! (See **what if**).

With Rhinos you will very definitely have to introduce **lifeboat clauses** to protect yourself from *fait accompli* as it is no good to you when they have delivered 80% of what was agreed and they simply raise their hands and say 'that's life, *'force majeure'*, or 'it's out of my hands.'

If they have made public statements about their position to their own side or to the public at the beginning of the negotiation then you are going to have to spend time trying to build a way out of their own traps for them. This means putting yourself in their shoes and trying to think of ways to sell any deal to their constituents. See **Golden Bridge** and **Acceptance speech**.

Common Tricks & Tactics of a Rhino

All of the following tricks and tactics are in the second part of this book, listed alphabetically: *Always say No, Commitment ploy, Culture A – "that's the way we do things round here", Hands tied, Non-negotiable/un-discussable, Playing a broken record, Standard terms, Stonewalls, "That might be the case where you come from but....", Walk out, "We've never done that before", Minimum Order.*

8. Tortoise

Common Characteristics

Tortoises are slow, armoured, ugly creatures that somehow manage to survive beyond the lifespan of most other animals. It's hard to get past their defences and when they do bite into something it can be hard to get them to let go.

The Tortoise negotiator is deliberately slow. They use delaying tactics such as going off on tangents, asking for breaks, telling you that they will think about it and get back to you, etc. They are doing this, of course, to use time against you. This will especially be the case if you have a deadline or even if you both have deadlines (as they are masters at brinkmanship). They understand that when time drags out, impatient and inexperienced negotiators get worried and stressed and are likely to make concessions just to get the ball rolling again.

They may pretend to be slow of hearing or mind to get you to repeat over and over your position. They do this to try and find flaws and weaknesses in your arguments, to show you that they are aware of your tricks, or simply to wear you down.

They may pretend not to speak your language and use an interpreter. That way they can observe you while you are talking to the interpreter and not to them. They will also only remember information that suits them and conveniently forget things that don't. They may also only perceive what they want to.

They will also use silence against you knowing that more often than not the first person who speaks after a protracted period of silence is the one who makes concessions. Some cultures such as the Japanese and Finnish pause before replying to absorb what you have said and there are many anecdotes of people from cultures where silence is uncomfortable making concessions to the Japanese just to fill the silence. A Tortoise negotiator does this as a negotiation tactic, not as part of their culture.

You may find that you rush to make a deal in the limousine on the way back out to the airport. It is at those times that you suddenly discover that they are very far from stupid and that in fact their hearing is absolutely perfect. However, you may find in some cultures that this is also a test of your interest and commitment and that it is not a negotiating tactic to wear you down. Needless to say, some background reading on the culture you are dealing with will go a long way to tipping you off about their intentions if you find yourself up against someone who appears to be a Tortoise.

One of the cardinal rules in streetwise negotiating according to many negotiators is to pretend that you are less than you are. The belief is that this will lull others into a false sense of confidence and they will not be as careful. Of course, there are cultures where it is important to display a strong confident image in a negotiation but it is very easy for Tortoises to take advantage of that, using the ego of people in that culture against them.

In the case of the Tortoise negotiator it is almost as if their heart beats slower than yours at times and it can become very frustrating dealing with them. You will pay the price for your impatience though, so take a deep breath and slow down.

How to deal with a Tortoise Negotiator

When negotiating with a Tortoise you have to be patient. If you are travelling to another country be prepared to stay for longer, perhaps by not buying a return ticket, or simply realising that you may have to come back several times before a deal is closed.

If you are dealing with people who use silence against you then relax and simply count inside your head. Every time you reach fifty congratulate yourself for not having rushed in with a concession to fill the silence.

Avoid letting them know if you have deadlines and, even better, try to avoid having deadlines in the first place (communicate this clearly to your superiors if you feel it is a tactic being used against you). If the slow speed of a negotiation is part of the culture you may simply have to accept that there will be a long period of 'getting to know each other' and that when trust has been established the pace may accelerate considerably, perhaps even leaving you caught out by the sudden change in gears.

Be very careful of treating the other person as stupid, regardless of how they act. It is highly unlikely that you will actually be negotiating with someone who really has no idea, unless they are very young and inexperienced and then you may find that they become even pricklier if you treat them like a fool (unless of course your preferred negotiation style is that of the Tiger negotiator and you find the tactic of destroying the other person works for you).

You can only really see who has been foolish when the final contract has been written and very often even then you will not know as a Tortoise will praise you for having done so well against them and declare that they have won nothing out of the negotiation. You should know your strategy and position very well and everyone on your team should be aware of it also because if you are bluffing and asked to repeat your position repeatedly by a Tortoise you may tie yourself in knots trying to remember what you have said before.

If you see that the other side are slowing down then try to figure out why it is in their interest to go slow. You should temporarily go slow as well and evaluate the situation. You may have to decide to create 'false deadlines' to force them up against to speed up the process if you feel that they are simply buying time. Sometimes you are not really dealing with a Tortoise but with someone that is actually negotiating with a third party and simply using their negotiations with you to put the squeeze on the other group. In this case they are in effect wasting your time and money.

Common Tricks & Tactics of a Tortoise

All of the following tricks and tactics are in the second part of this book, listed alphabetically: *Asking questions when you already know the answer, Brinkmanship, Buy Time to Think, Consult with the pillow, Deadlock, Delaying ploy, I'll think about it and get back to you later, "I'm sorry, I've made a mistake, I'm only a simple foreigner, Interpreter, Lost in translation, My hearing isn't very good, Patience, Playing dumb, Stalling for concession, Stamina, Two translators.*

9. Baboon

Common Characteristics

Aggressive, screaming, posturing, angry. That's a baboon for you. Also synonym in many places for 'idiot'. Nowhere are baboons associated with class, decorum and mature reflection.

Negotiating with a blustering Baboon can be particularly tiring. They will use emotion as a weapon against you, ranting and raving, interrupting, getting angry over the slightest insult, complaining and whining out loud, throwing up their arms in despair at every proposal from your side and even walking out regularly from the meeting only to return later and start off again.

They may make excessive demands above and below your offer (high and low balling) and escalate dramatically their demands at the slightest provocation. They may try to surprise you at different points in the negotiation with dramatic proposals to unnerve you. They will try and rush you at the end into taking a hurried (and generally unwise) decision. They may try and overwhelm you with a mountain of information that you cannot possibly hope to analyse in the time they are giving you. And it is very possible that they will sulk if you get serious with them.

They are masters at using unpredictability and irrationality which unsettles anyone who has to negotiate with them and means that you are desperate to bring the negotiation to a close as quickly as possible just to get away from them (and that hurried eagerness to finish means there is a greater chance that you will make mistakes.)

Natural Baboons are already difficult to deal with but if you happen to be dealing with one that is fully aware of what they are doing and using it as a deliberate tactic then they can be very dangerous. Their behaviour might be to gain all the benefits of a Natural Baboon but they may also be creating that impression so you do not take them seriously and you drop your guard, not expecting them to be calculating Snakes behind it all.

How to deal with a Baboon Negotiator

Stop and take a deep breath. You might be dealing with tactics, culture or a petulant child. Really getting angry will not solve anything here. You might find that you have to raise your voice initially to he heard but once you have matched them then lead them to a quieter tone of voice and a calmer attitude. (See **Mirroring and Pacing**)

Be very careful of being provoked. If you get angry they might accuse you of insulting them and walk away from the negotiation. To restart the negotiations you have to make a concession. Or else they walk away from the negotiations and later you discover that they were losing on a particular point and they wanted to end the negotiations before they lost more (but of course they want to blame you for being the cause). And of course there is also the fact that when you are angry you are not thinking clearly and make mistakes.

You might decide that you want to get angry as your own tactic - but make sure that it is a tactic and that your mind is still rational inside. Go slowly when they start to act like a Baboon. Generally this behaviour is to prevent you from thinking clearly about what is being discussed, and to change subjects. Rarely does matching them improve the situation unless you are momentarily trying to mirror and then pace them to a calmer rhythm.

Common Tricks & Tactics of a Baboon

All of the following tricks and tactics are in the second part of this book, listed alphabetically: *Anger faking, Anger provoking, Blowfish, Bluff, Crazy power, Escalation, Hustle close, Shock opening, Yelling and screaming, Surprize, Proximity.*

10. Owl

Common Characteristics

For millennia the Owl has been a symbol of wisdom, justice and libraries full of books. Of course if you are a mouse, an Owl is a terrifying predator with a sharp beak and flashing claws. For the sake of argument we will assume that you are not a mouse reading this book. However it is a good idea to keep that alternative image in mind. That way you will not be completely taken in by the austere face that does both 'sleepy' and 'surprized' equally well and a head that can turn around and see the world from both sides.

We have chosen the Owl as the symbol of the negotiator that approaches negotiations with an air of fairness and an attitude of "compromise". They will use expressions like 'I think this is a fair offer', 'in the interest of fairness', 'how about we split the difference', 'I give you my word on that', 'Honestly,..', 'I think we should meet somewhere in the middle', 'It's only fair to expect...', 'We should both give up something, don't you think?'.

They will go for the 'fifty-fifty' approach every time. They believe in putting all their cards on the table and finding a solution that is "fair" for everyone. Sounds a lot like an Eagle in fact. They have a clear idea of what fairness means – to them. If this differs to what you believe to be fair then they may start slipping into other negotiation styles – the Rhino or the Porcupine, for example. They do this because they believe you are being difficult, not because they feel you have a different perception of the situation.

While 'fair' solutions can also seem to be fast and straightforward for everyone concerned they are not always the best solutions. Sometimes an element of creativity has to be used to come up with less straightforward solutions and this is one area where the Owl falls down.

Their emphasis on 'fair' can also end up with them breaking a deal rather than accepting one because they perceive it to be 'unfair'. In an ideal world that is a great approach but in the world of negotiations that would end up in a lot of broken deals as 'fairness' does not always come into the equation. Sometimes you have to accept the deal as the best one that is on the table, given the circumstances, and taking into account that what you are being offered is better than your alternative away from the table. The answer of a competitive negotiator (especially a Tiger or Elephant) would be:

'Yes, I think it is *fair* that we split the deal 50/50 but as I have all the power and resources and you desperately need this deal then I think a figure of 80/20 is more *appropriate*.'

There is also one other point you should be aware of – the Owl Style is often a style that other negotiating styles (e.g. Chimpanzees or Snakes) adopt externally to lull you into a false sense of security.

You should also remember that very often if someone has to say that they or the deal is fair then the opposite is in often the case.

Be very careful of the expression 'let's split the difference.' This *sounds* fair but always remember that the person who set the last price/position is the one who has effectively decided where the middle point is. If you say 10 and they say 20 then they have decided that the middle point is 15. If instead they respond to your initial 10 with 30 then they have decided that the middle point is 20. This move is carried out by a Toucan passing itself off as an Owl.

They may also say 'let's put our cards on the table' to find the middle point. You will notice that you are the one who puts the cards on the table first and they know more about you than you do about them. However they will continue to give off an appearance of being wise and impartial.

They may also simply have the reputation of being an Owl and live off their expert and fair status while in their heart of hearts they are only an Owl when it suits them. Having the reputation of being an Owl does not mean that they will continue to be fair with you and certainly does not mean they are an expert on everything.

Be wary of Chimpanzees wearing Owl feathers!

How to deal with an Owl Negotiator

With an Owl you should be careful about thinking they are an expert, or fair *all* the time. Always ask the question 'why is this fair?' if they use the statement that it is. Look at the small print in every contract because you might find that they are hiding little items there in the hope that you will not look for them, believing them to be 'wise and fair'. If they act insulted that you are questioning their integrity then simply say that it is company policy and you have to do it with all contracts. If you do find sections inserted in the contract or if you find that the objective criteria they are using is not in fact very objective then act as if a mistake has been made. You will find that they make less 'mistakes' after this.

Be wary of superficially fair 'split the difference' offers and simple solutions as rarely will they make them when it benefits you and hurts them.

However, it also pays not to become too paranoid either. There are magnanimous people out there and very often when the deal is not that important or what you are haggling over represents a very small part of the deal then compromising and splitting the difference can make perfect sense rather than wasting more time and resources by haggling over every cent.

If you feel that you are dealing with a true Owl you should always think about what is necessary to make your proposal 'sound and look fair' given the perception of fairness that the other negotiator has (or the ruling conventions of fairness in that culture at the time).   As mentioned earlier – if they perceive the deal as unfair, they may not sign, even if it is in their best interest to do so.

Common Tricks & Tactics of an Owl

All of the following tricks and tactics are in the second part of this book, listed alphabetically: *Compromise, Fair, Reputation, Split the difference, WYSIWIG, X-ray, Zero extras, Cards on the table.*

11. Chameleon

Common Characteristics

They adapt and they change. When people think of a chameleon they do not normally start with the little swivel eyes and the long tail. They start with the fact that it changes colours. And they do this to blend in with the background. They want to blend into the background to make it more difficult for predators to catch them. They change so they cannot be caught. Their negotiator namesakes follow the same philosophy.

It can be very frustrating dealing with a Chameleon as you expend a lot of energy simply trying to tie them down and find out exactly what their point or objective is. You negotiate happily around a certain range of issues, make concessions and compromises and then discover that they have moved the goalposts and they actually want something else, though they will happily take everything you have given up to that point.

Very often, just before you have closed the deal they will make last minute changes which appear innocent but later prove to be in their favour. When sending contracts back and forth always make sure to check everything carefully as they may make changes that they are hoping you will not notice.

They may also change their behaviour regularly so that you never really know who you are dealing with: 'Doctor Jekyll or Mr. Hyde.' They may switch negotiators regularly so that you cannot get an idea of who you are really dealing with, though they will be sure to have a clear picture of you passed on to the next negotiator. This may be a simple change of person or you being passed up the corporate ladder. You will then have to be sure that you stay on message and that you do not give away a new piece of information each time you deal with another person.

How to deal with a Chameleon Negotiator

It is essential with a Chameleon to clearly define their interests in the opening stages of the negotiation. Write down what they are saying and before you advance agree that you have understood everything they have said. Confirm at this point that there are no other issues. Later when you are putting forward your proposal base everything on the issues you have heard from them. Make sure that they understand that if those issues change then whatever you are offering will also change. This is why it is a good idea to use conditional language as you are not tying yourself to a particular position until they have confirmed that the deal is possible. ('We would be prepared to give way on that issue if you also respond in kind with a concession on the issue of the access rights.')

It is also important to identify early on if the person you are dealing with has the authority to take a decision and if not then who does. If you understand that they are not the final decision maker then be careful of making any concessions until you actually feel that they will be reciprocated. Simply suggest that a different package might be possible and you would be prepared to discuss them with someone who has the authority to take a decision. However you should be careful of alienating the person who you are dealing with as their superior may never hear of your fantastic offer. Therefore you will have to convince them that it is in their interest that the agreement happens, without making any concessions to them.

You should use the law of consistency with Chameleons:

'If I understood you correctly earlier then you said.....'

'Sorry, how does that fit with your earlier position...?'

'Perhaps, I'm a little confused, didn't you ......?'

'Maybe we should just go back and look at what we agreed earlier.....'

This can be very powerful because if they decide to be obviously inconsistent then they will lose credibility and authority in the negotiation, both of which are important in any deal making situation (it is more important to be trusted than to be liked).

Common Tricks & Tactics of a Chameleon

All of the following tricks and tactics are in the second part of this book, listed alphabetically: *Change the goal posts, Changing seats at the table, Changing the standards, Circumstances have changed, It's a deal, let's negotiate, Last minute Changes, Musical Chairs, Rollercoaster, Sudden changes of behaviour, Surprize.*

12. Toucan

Common Characteristics

The Toucans are associated with being able to mimic humans speaking and they have a big beak. Clever animals, but not as beautiful as the Flamingo.

Toucan negotiators use language and their skill with it as a tool against you in a negotiation. Wordplay, programmed responses, confusion, logic traps, hypnotic language – that's the Toucan. They do not necessarily lle and they do not attack you. They do not shout at you and they do not sit on you. They wrap you in a cocoon of verbosity that cushions you in cotton wool until you are signing the contract with the same expression on your face as someone who has just had pixie dust thrown in their eyes.

They use lines such as 'is that your best offer?' or simply 'you'll have to do better than that' which trap you into giving more or risk ending the negotiation – all without giving anything away themselves.

They also use tricks such as 'how would you like to pay for that?' or 'in what colour will you be taking it? These come under the umbrella term 'assumptive close' where they use language that suggests that you have already agreed to the deal. Up to that point everything was possible, or perhaps improbable, but suddenly they have shifted the language into definite statements.

They use key words like 'free', 'because', 'only', 'guaranteed', 'safe', 'investment' in all the right places as they know these words elicit positive responses in potential clients.

They suggest offers in a way that makes you feel like you will definitely be getting something but when you actually think about what they are saying you realise that nothing has been guaranteed. 'We might be able to arrange that.' 'We could certainly look into that.' 'We would be open to considering that.' Etc.

They will also use embedded controllers. This is where you use the imperative after a non-imperative suggestion or request. However they make the tiniest of pauses before using the imperative so your body often reacts reflexively to the imperative but your mind hears the request or the suggestion and doesn't take offence. For example:

> 'Would you like to (request, *pause*) buy it now (imperative)?'

'If I were you I would (*pause*) take it for a test run.'

'Could you (*pause*) think of three reasons why this could be the model for you?

This is an effective technique where the imperative is hidden in a sentence that makes it sound innocent but by modulating the person's voice and pausing in the correct place they are able to use the imperative regularly with you.

They also use the double bind technique where they give you a choice of two options, both of which suit them. This is a step up from the assumptive close:

'Would you like that delivered today or tomorrow?'

'Will you be ordering that in red or in green?

They use commitment traps to lock you into a decision. This works by asking you seemingly innocuous questions where you give standard answers. However they have built the questions in a way that locks you into a logic that provides them with the answer that suits them:

'So, you feel that this pipeline is essential in this area.'

Yes.

'And you have stated that you trust us to do the job well.'

Yes.

> 'And you have agreed that we cannot do it for free and that safety is a priority.'

> Yes.

> 'Then you must agree that the 5% coverage on the insurance is a must. As you've said yourself, we cannot take that from our fees or we will be operating at below our own bottom line.'

Sometimes they ask you to make small commitments and make inconsequential requests of you to get you in a compliant and giving mood before bringing in their bigger requests. You may find yourself agreeing to things that under normal circumstances you wouldn't.

They will use visualisation techniques such as:

> 'Imagine yourself, sitting behind your desk, and switching on this beauty and it just revs into life and you can feel the power. And then the screen switches on instantly and you are presented with the clearest graphics that exist on any model. You can see your holiday photos as if you were there on the beach again. Now imagine a whole row of those models in your office and every person there turning to smile at you and give you the thumbs up.'

They understand that when you follow their hypnotic visualisation your body's muscles involuntarily follow through the motions of what they are saying. Once that happens it is more difficult to say No to what they are offering.

They will tell success stories about other people that gradually convert into you and while you are busy imagining yourself as the protagonist in the story (and not concentrating on what you are doing, a classic trick of hypnotists) they will have you signing the contract. You may even find yourself repeating verbatim the story to your spouse and seven children when you park that two seater sports car in the drive of the family home.

How to deal with a Toucan Negotiator

With a toucan your best strategy is to use active listening. Carefully listen to everything they are really saying, not what you think they are saying. Repeat and clarify constantly. Remember what your goals were when you entered the negotiation.

Make sure to take a break to look over what they are offering you, especially by using numbers instead of words to see what their proposal is, without the sizzle. You might have to play stupid here but it is better to look stupid in the negotiation than to be seduced by their honey tongues and regret later.

Make sure to look at all the possible meanings of any contract they offer you and to have a lawyer or expert explain to you any obscure or unusual expressions. Remember the expression 'Nothing is agreed until everything is agreed.'

Common Tricks & Tactics of a Toucan

All of the following tricks and tactics are in the second part of this book, listed alphabetically: *As you consider the benefits of ..... you might like to...., Assumptive close, Awareness directors, Because, By-the-way, Commitment traps, Double bind, Embedded commands, Experience shows that..., "Give it to me straight", "Help me out this time and I'll see you right next time", "I'd love to but", "I'm not going to tell you, "Is that your best offer?", "Is that the best you can do?", It's ok not to...., Labelling, "Let me see what I can do", Let me tell you a story, People like you, Perry Mason Ploy, Power of Only, Question tags, References to how unimportant this deal is to you, Rephrased negative, Rosy future, Silver line it, Softener, The more you...., The more you, Try and fail, Vague language, Vague modals, Visualisation, You'll have to do better than that...., Your friend John already drives one, "9.99 it", Just because it's you, Give me your best price, Logic traps.*

13.Porcupine

Common Characteristics

Porcupines shouldn't really be in the jungle, though they are less defenceless than their Penguin and Ostrich counterparts. Just like their animal counterparts they wander through the trees oblivious to the danger they might be in and when they encounter opposition they become prickly as hell.

The porcupine is in the avoidance group. They dislike negotiations as they treat them as a source of conflict and are terrified of being cheated, manipulated or being pressurised. You have to treat them with kid's gloves or they will go sullen and silent or break off the negotiations. They will give non-committal answers until you change your tone and you may find that you are making concessions just to put them at ease. You may also find that you give up on the negotiation because you perceive it to be too much effort to engage them properly. Be careful of this style as it might in fact be a closet Baboon or Snake.

How to deal with a Porcupine Negotiator

With a porcupine you have to separate the people from the problem. Do not necessarily make concessions simply to make them happy. You should treat them carefully and well but keep the issues apart. Try to involve them from the beginning in creating the solution so they do not feel they are being pushed around or tricked. Explain the objective criteria you are using so that they can see where your proposal is coming from. Ask for their opinion at each step and encourage them to make comments.

If they get angry or upset then ask them what is bothering them in a non-accusatory tone of voice. Use active listening to find out what is really upsetting them and encourage them to talk about their issues. It is essential to build up trust with these people and eliminate their reasons for being so sensitive. If you have done your preparation correctly you should have some idea of what history and emotions they are bringing to the table, and by anticipating their issues and encouraging them to be open about them, then you may defuse them.

Common Tricks & Tactics of a Porcupine

Sulking, sniping, withdrawal, turning into a three year old child when you try to get them to go to bed. The following tricks and tactics are in the second part of this book: *Culture B - what you're saying/asking for is offensive here, Hurt and betrayed.*

14. Vulture

Common Characteristics

Can you see them, the vultures? Spiralling over you, watching every move you make, waiting for you to die, worn out, so they can drift down on a burning breeze and pick at your bones. The Vulture is a cold hearted negotiator, wearing you down with facts and figures and numbers and picking through everything with their beady eyes, looking for ways to trap you.

The vulture uses information as a weapon. They bring in officially neutral third party experts; engineers, lawyers and accounts to overwhelm you with information. They try to control the agenda, knowing that only what is on it can be discussed.

They will set themselves up as an expert on the issues being discussed and then extend that legitimacy and authority into other areas without you realising. When they have established their credibility they may then bring in false or incomplete information that you do not check.

They may also bring in officially objective information and benchmarks that you would do well to check before taking them as the de facto reference points. They understand the power of having things in writing and will bring most of their information typed and printed. This does not make the information any truer than if it was spoken but people are still influenced more by the written word than by the spoken.

They will manipulate numbers and statistics so that you have to be very careful that you are not confused by all their calculations. They will also cherry pick from all your competitors' offers so it looks like they are referencing actual market conditions but this is not strictly true as no single offer matches the one they are presenting you with.

They will insist on writing the contract and you should be very careful of this, especially with the small print as you may find that there are exceptions and extras added in that were never agreed in the actual negotiation itself. If you write the contract they will find a thousand exceptions with it and take it apart.

How to deal with a Vulture Negotiator

You will need experts of your own when dealing with a Vulture. Do not bluff as they will pick everything apart that you say. Be able to explain all your numbers and justify them if necessary.

You should also be prepared to go through every line of the contract as they will play with numbers and legal jargon to confuse you, in the hope that you do not have the time, knowledge or energy to go through everything. Always make sure that you understand and agree with their 'objective criteria'.   If you are not happy with the criteria they are proposing then say so. You should have your own objective criteria prepared as well so that you can compare and contrast and fight for the criteria that you believe to be most applicable.

Common Tricks & Tactics of a Vulture

All of the following tricks and tactics are in the second part of this book, listed alphabetically: *Blind with science/numbers, Exceptions, Expert, Funny money, Information, Lawyer, Magic writing, Nibbling, "Only 40 cents a day", Overwhelm, Persist and don't desist, Power of Confusion, Salami (slicing), Sweeten this deal, Take notes, Third party experts, "We should have been told", We can change that later, Writing the contract, Email.*

15. Ostrich

Common Characteristics

The ostrich is the classic avoider. They do not like negotiations and will try to avoid them at all cost. When they sense anything like conflict they will run a mile. It can be difficult to find them and when you do they may not want to discuss the issue at hand. They can do this by changing the subject or using humour to avoid taking the subject seriously.

How to deal with an Ostrich Negotiator

Go slowly, get them involved and build on their points. Don't go off on pleasant tangents that avoid the subject. It is your responsibility to make sure that the negotiation advances (though try to do so nicely so they won't simply run from the negotiation).

Do not impose strict timelines on them but when they have agreed use the consistency principle with them and remind them of what they have agreed. Do not use Tiger tactics with them if you want to work with them in future as they will simply avoid doing business with you, feeling that no matter how good the possible agreement is they could not deal with your aggressive behaviour on a regular basis.

Common Tricks & Tactics of an Ostrich

Rather than a trick, their strategy is to avoid at all costs anything that smells of a negotiation. They will buy or not at the first price and spend more time looking for better alternatives than trying to talk down the one they have in front of them.

If they are selling then they will say that they 'will come back to you' if the deal is not good enough for them and then you will never hear from them again. Meanwhile they will change their route home and avoid all coffee shops where they think you might take a break.

16. Eagle

This majestic king of birds soars high above the earth, looking at the world unfold beneath it, dispassionately and objectively.

The Eagle negotiator tries to do the same. They look at the bigger picture and try to find creative solutions that will satisfy both sides. They try to see the negotiation as a positive sum game where all parties at the table come away with more than they had before the negotiation started.

This side will make an effort to avoid mixing the people with the issues being discussed: They don't let the other side use their personalities to influence the deal and they do their best not to take things personally. Their motto is to be soft on the people but hard on the issues. They do their best to avoid being visibly provoked rather than responding to insults with insults or aggression with aggression. They aim to maintain a cordial, helpful working relationship while remaining firm in their determination to achieve their goals.

They focus on interests, as opposed to positions. This means that instead of accepting the fact that you want to pay 10,000 for a car they want to find out *why* you want the car. They will spend time trying to discover what your interests are so that they can find a solution that is based on those interests and not simply stating an alternative position and then trying to haggle towards a middle point.

They will avoid using dirty tricks as they do not think this will help a long term relationship between you and them. They believe in a deal that will last instead of taking advantage of you at every opportunity.

They will ask you to justify your position and explain what criteria you used, as they have spent time putting together their own proposal with objective standards, norms and information. This means they are more interested in getting the equivalent of a 'fair' deal, one that can be justified, than everything they might be able to get if they were to bluff and inflate their offer.

For them power comes through legitimacy and strong alternatives to the negotiation at hand. This means they will spend time discovering precedents, industry standards, third party sources and references etc. It also means that they will develop what is called a BATNA in the world of negotiations. BATNA stands for Best Alternative To a Negotiated Agreement. Your BATNA is your best option available if you get up in the middle of a negotiation and walk out. If you are unemployed and you have two job interviews on the same day at the same time then before you choose you have two alternatives. However the moment you decide to do one interview you forfeit the other. When you are in the interview, your BATNA is to go back to being unemployed. An Eagle Negotiator would spend time developing their BATNA. In this case it would mean changing the time of the interviews so that you can go to both so that your BATNA continues to be 'accepting the other job' rather than being unemployed. The better your BATNA, the greater your power in the negotiation.

They will spend time brainstorming and problem solving, not only with their own team but with you, to try and find creative and imaginative solutions to apparent deadlocks where all sides concerned can benefit.

They try to reframe problems and proposals in a way that both sides understand and can accept. This also involves focusing on improving communication rather than muddying it.

They accept that sometimes a deal is not possible but that through clear communication this can be discovered earlier and time is saved. Naturally, they also believe that all negotiations, with or without a deal being reached, should conclude on a positive note so the relationship between the negotiators is not damaged. This means that if circumstances change there will be no impediments to negotiating again with the same people in future.

How to deal with an Eagle Negotiator

You should constantly test to see if they are genuine as they might simply be pretending to be 'fair' and lying about their interests to create a false sense of trust with you. In fact one of the dangers for true Eagle Negotiators are competitive negotiators – Snakes, Chimpanzees, Vultures - masquerading as Eagles and taking advantage of their desire to share information to find common or complementary interests. An unscrupulous negotiator can simply invent "objective standards" of their own to argue their case and will search the Eagle's open policy for weaknesses and vulnerabilities which they can then exploit.

The effectiveness and fairness of an Eagle style can smash into the ground when the negotiation involves parties that will never see each other again, where the accepted culture of the particular negotiation is haggling (in some Bazaars, enquiring about the interests of the other side will simply be met with lies), and with inexperienced negotiators who ruin a potentially good deal because they cannot escape the restrictions of their preferred animal style (e.g. natural baboons). In these cases the negotiation may simply break down.

If the deal is going to be long term or if you are going to have to do business with them regularly then your best choice is to adopt the same style as the Eagle and try to find a solution that is beneficial to you both and that will be long lasting.

Common Tricks & Tactics of an Eagle

All of the following tricks and tactics are in the second part of this book, listed alphabetically: *Acceptance Speech, Acknowledge, Appreciate, Back off, Balanced Team, BATNA baby!, Brainstorm, Conditional concessions, Control Expectations, Establish the rules of the game, Ethos, Explain to me why..., Flexibility, Follow-up, Golden Bridge, Help me to help you, "Help me to understand", If I could show you, would you?, Increase the size of the pie, Know where you're going, Legitimate power, Let them own the solution, Let them save face, Lifeboat clause, Linking, Listening, Mutual solutions, Never talk down, Nothing agreed until everything is agreed, Objective standards, Open on a positive note, Package, Perspective taking, Phasing, Positive end note, Post-op, Precedents, Prepare!, Prioritize, Problem solving questions, Process not result, Referencing a benchmark, Reframe, Rehearse, Respect, Rest, Separate people from the problem, Summarise, Test assumptions, Thank you, The perfect solution/magic wand, There is more than one way to skin a cat, Trust, Turn things upside down, Understand perception, Understand power, Understanding value differentiation, Waterbed it, What if?, Why not?, "If I remember correctly", "Let me check my notes...".*

4oo+

Tricks and Tactics to
Help You Survive

The original goal of this book was to help Penguins and Ostriches become Eagles, and to give Eagles a better idea of what they are facing when they fly low in the jungle. The world of negotiations is a dangerous place and full of many unscrupulous, and sometimes vicious, characters. To defend yourself against their attacks you must learn what those attacks are. Therefore many of the following tricks and tactics are not ones that we suggest you use, but we do strongly advise you study them to better protect yourself.

We are aware that some of those unscrupulous characters we have already mentioned are reading this book in the hope that they can become even better at eating Penguin Pie. Our belief is that people who use dirty tricks are generally aware of them already and will gain less from these pages than those people who are acting in good faith and want to learn more. It certainly isn't our intention to commit the moral equivalent of giving a machinegun to a monkey.

In the different tricks and tactics we have regularly stated that 'studies show...'. You can find more details on these studies in the "Notes" section at the end of the book. You will also be able to find further information in the books listed in the "Select Bibliography" section.

In the first part of this book, 'The Negotiation Jungle', we have identified the most common tricks for each animal style. We leave it up you to decide if you think the Eagle is a more ethical negotiator than the Tiger, Snake or Vulture or if you would prefer to be a Porcupine or a Rhino. You may take this decision based on your own personality or on the negotiating style you feel you currently use. However you may also decide to adopt a particular style having read the descriptions of the different animals. We cannot take that decision for you. Having taken that decision you can interpret the 400+ tactics and tricks accordingly. It is, however, our sincere hope that you use the knowledge in the following pages to protect yourself, and not to attack others, and that from now on this knowledge helps you achieve better, bigger and more efficient results in every negotiation you enter.

Read on. Enjoy. Learn. Improve.

Good luck.

A

---

1. **Acceptance Speech**:

   When you are negotiating with the other side you should think of their constituents, their stakeholders and especially their bosses (who might be someone as simple as their spouse, or something as complicated as a board of directors that then has to get the agreement passed at a shareholder's meeting). Think of who they will have to convince that they have reached a good deal with you (you are the external negotiation, but chances are that they will have an internal negotiation afterwards).

   Imagine the acceptance speech for the deal with you that they will give in their company. If it is not a good one then don't expect them to go for your deal. If *you* can write a good acceptance speech then it will be easier for them to mentally write that speech as you are selling, ('if I was your boss I would be delighted at the savings you are going to make' being a pretty blunt example). Helping them will help build a relationship with them in future.

   Of course if you are a competitive negotiator then focus on getting them to sign the contract, don't let them see the small print and do not worry if they get executed when they bring the signed contract back to their company/spouse. Not great for building a healthy relationship, though.

2. **Acknowledge:**

Simply recognising that the other side has a valid point or even that their view point makes sense given the parameters they are working within is a good way of persuading them later to listen to your good idea. When you acknowledge you can add the proviso of 'given the information they have', 'the angle they are looking at ', or 'taking into account their position'. So much of the time we feel that others aren't listening to us, or don't understand us, that we feel we have to explain ourselves and defend our position (sometimes ad nauseam). As a result instead of listening to our counterpart's offer or looking for a solution we spend our time digging trenches around our position. When the other side acknowledges us and our point of view (and does so sincerely, not simply 'yeah, I see what you mean, yawn.') we stop digging trenches and start to look over at what they are doing.

3. **Alcohol:**

When people are drinking they do silly things. For many people that includes not knowing when to keep their mouths shut. It also makes them happy (at least temporarily) and makes them like the other person (at least temporarily). When they are drunk they do not think clearly.

As negotiators, when we like people, can't keep our mouths closed and don't think clearly we make bad decisions. Our little angel negotiator tells us to be careful of getting drunk, plan for it and concentrate on keeping subjects close to neutral subjects, unrelated to the negotiation, if it happens. Our little devil negotiator tells us to get the other side drunk and find out as much information from them as possible.

4. **Always say No:**

There are people who are positive and always looking for the next adventure. There are other people whose default setting is 'answer No immediately to any proposal, no matter how good it may sound'. For people like this it is better to be safe with what they have than risk getting something new that may or may not be better than what they already have. However there are others who simply use this as a tactic in a negotiation. If you say 'No' to people who are desperate or very interested in doing business with you it can make you seem even more appealing. For them, when they hear 'no' they may feel that they have to change their offer, generally for the better, to try and get a yes from you.

There are classic experiments that show that children are indifferent when having to choose between two different toys until the experiments make it slightly more difficult to get one of the toys. Automatically the children want the more difficult to get toy. Adults are not much different. Everyone wants a two seat sports car until they get one and they wonder where they can put the shopping bags!

I have seen cases where simply repeating 'No' encourages the seller to compete against his previous offers to try and please the customer. It is always better to find out the reasons behind the 'No' before even considering changing your proposal.

5. **Anchoring**:

When you do not have a clear idea about the correct value/price of something you can fall prey to anchoring. If you walk into a shop thinking that barbecues should have a price of $150 a piece then you will negotiate around that price.   If they start by telling you the average price of a toilet seat is $9,000 then you can do one of two things. The sensible thing: go and ask in other shops to find out if this is in fact a standard price for toilets. The less sensible thing: negotiate around this new anchor and buy a god value toilet at $7,000.

With a toilet bowl it can be easy to ascertain the asking price as you simply check it out on the internet or go to another shop as the example indicates.   However for a complicated project or service where there is no ready comparison it can be easy to be unbalanced by whatever anchor price you are given.   Very often there is no catalogue where you can compare. In this case if you have been anchored to a particular price you may indeed haggle them down or up a lot, but always from the base that they have provided.

In a principled negotiation these anchors will be based on objective criteria. In a competitive negotiation these anchors might be random numbers designed to see if they can get away with as much as possible, or to shock you into changing your expectations.

6. **Adding and subtracting:**

Make sure that you have a product or service that has things that can be added and subtracted. This avoids you haggling purely about the price. 'Fine, we can drop the price but that will mean the product is delivered in 10 days, not 3.' 'Well, if you are prepared to pay that little bit extra we can guarantee a one-day delivery service.' Adding and subtracting is what negotiating is all about. Before you enter a negotiation make sure you know how to do the simple maths of a good deal.

7. **Anger faking:**

Why would someone ever fake being angry in a negotiation? Easy, it gets results. You can fake anger by way of indignation (demand apology, apology equals concession) or fake anger in order to intimidate (my anger is so visible you back down on whatever you are asking for, or you make a concession that wasn't even requested, simply to try and appease the other, or fake anger to use this as an excuse to abandon the negotiation.

How do you deal with this? Before you make any apology ask yourself whether the other person is justified or not. Just because they act angry doesn't mean that A) they are or B) it should affect you C) you're actually responsible.

8. **Anger provoking:**

Anger is an emotion that changes our perception of reality. It reduces our wider vision, sometimes in not seeing the wider picture and sometimes in that we focus in on the object of our anger in front of us to the exclusion of everything else. It makes us act in ways that we would not normally if we were thinking clearly.

Nature was wise to create the emotion of anger. That burst of rage could give us the required boost of adrenaline and strength to bludgeon a sabre tooth tiger to death and thus survive. We have maintained that ability to get irrationally angry from cave men days but in today's world there are few occasions in a negotiation where you would be forgiven for bludgeoning your counterpart to death with a club.

In the modern world getting angry (and not controlling it) means that you stop thinking clearly, act defensively, attack when you should pause, offend the other side in actions or words (and then have to make a concession by way of apology) or perhaps storm out of the negotiation (which may suit the other side – now you are to blame for the negotiation being wrecked.).

You can fake anger if that is part of your strategy, you can use angry indignation to steer you correctly and defend values that are dear to you, but be very careful of getting angry because you have been manipulated. Stop. Count to ten. Take a deep breath. If you don't calm down after that then ask to be excused while you go to the bathroom and bludgeon the hand drier to death with a club!

9. **Answering a question with a question:**
Getting information on/from the other side is a must. So therefore asking questions is a must in a negotiation. In some competitive negotiations not giving the other side any information is a plus. All of these together make answering a question with a question a good policy. Some people are experts at it, and find it especially easy with people who really want to talk about themselves.

More experienced negotiators may insist on you answering their question first. They may simply say that it is your turn to answer some questions.

'Someone said that you always answer a question with a question, is that true?'

'Who told you that?'

10. **Apparent choice:**
With children it can be more effective to say 'which ones do you want to put on today, your red shoes or your blue shoes?' Instead of 'Put on your shoes!' Apparent choice gives power to the decider. When they feel in control they feel better about the final decision. Of course, afterwards they don't remember that the choice was presented to

them by you and was rigged from the beginning to suit your objectives.

'Would you like to pay in cash or by credit card?'

Come back with 'I was actually hoping to get it for free.'

See **Double Bind** and the extreme version, **Russian Front**.

11. **"Appeal to your better nature":**
    You appeal to their better nature to make concessions, donations, or a reduction in aggressive behaviour. Why would heartless negotiators ever do this? Well, because most negotiators are not heartless and it helps to remind them of this occasionally. If you are working for a charity or NGO this may be one of your negotiating tactics.

    This trick may look like it goes against the trick of self-interest but it feeds into the same thing. People don't want to feel bad. In other circumstances that might mean that they don't want to feel hungry, or conned, or lose out on an opportunity. But it can also include not wanting to feel guilty or bad about having done the wrong thing. If you have no power except this then you may have to use it – great if you use it with '**hurt and betrayed**', **pity** and **playing dumb.**

    If you are not a charity or an individual with a similar genuine claim to appealing to people's better nature, then be careful of using these tactics because if they are seen as simple negotiating ploys they can actually make the other side angry and more entrenched in their position.

12. **Appeal to their heart:**

People take a surprizing amount of decisions with their heart and then justify those decisions with their head.

> 'I love this car and I really want it. And besides it has great mileage and anyway, we need to spend more time together as a couple so it's great that there are no back seats for the kids.'

When putting forward a proposal never forget the emotional impact and emotional decision-making process going on inside the other person. Argue against their wants when it doesn't suit you at your peril but play up wants and recognise them when it does suit you. The other side might prefer the more expensive suit in bright green because they love green. It doesn't matter that most people choose the more practical blue suit at the cheaper price. That's fine, in this case tell them they will feel and look like a million dollars when they dress in avocado green. If it suits your interest don't dampen that emotional 'want', fan its flames.

13. **Appreciate:**

This is similar to **Acknowledge** but you say it in a slightly different way:

'I appreciate what you are saying AND (not but) given the information you have I understand where you are coming from. (Avoid *however* in this style) With the information we have/from our viewpoint we see things '*this way*'.

14. **Argue against yourself:**

    If you see the other side are wavering sometimes you can get them to commit by arguing against your own position:

    'Listen, you probably wouldn't want this anyway.'

    'No, I do, I do. It's just...'

    'The price? Am I asking for too much? You probably don't have that kind of money.'

    'No, the money is fine...'

    'The colour then, you don't like the red. I thought you might like another colour, it was just when you said you love cherries and love hearts, I thought...'

    'No, I love red.'

    'Well, if you insist, here's the contract and here's a pen.'

    At the very least you discount all the bad reasons and get to the real reasons.

15. **As you consider the benefits of ..... you might like to....:**

    This is part of the word tricks of Toucan negotiators. They have linked two ideas that you would never have thought of. First they are making you automatically focus on the benefits of their proposal, second they are then getting you to link your positive thoughts about their proposal to an **embedded command**.

    "As you consider the benefits of this extremely fast and expensive car you might like to think of our payment instalment plan."

16. **Ask for more:**
    Some people would consider this a basic of all negotiations. Whatever you are given you can always ask for more. They can do two things: 1. Say no. 2. Give you more. However you should be careful of being too cheeky in case they actually decide to walk away (this has more to do with how sensitive they are than with what you are asking for). Of course, if you have already squeezed every penny out of them there is a greater chance of this backfiring.

17. **Asking questions when you already know the answer:**
    I have an uncle that does this. He doesn't want to know the answer. He wants to know what you know, and what you think about a particular issue. When I was small I thought he knew very little about the world. It was only later that I realised that the opposite was true. In a negotiation that kind of realisation can be lethal –especially if it's combined with someone **playing dumb.**

18. **Assumptive close:**
    This is more common than you would believe, especially because when it is done smoothly and by an expert you don't realise what is happening. They deliberately assume that you have decided to buy when in fact you were still unsure. Examples include:
    'So, do you want that in red or blue?'
    'Will we deliver that on Monday or Tuesday?'
    'Do you want to pay by cash or by credit card?'

They assume you've closed and sometimes without realising, so do you.

19. **Avoid price:**
   Many negotiators prefer to avoid price at the beginning of the negotiation. It can be one of the more contentious issues in a negotiation (and very often what the other side has come to the table ready to defend and fight for). These negotiators prefer to get the ball rolling on easier issues - 'we'd like to start by looking at the issue of the colour of the bananas.'

20. **Awareness directors:**
   Sometimes you have to treat people like idiots. This is not because they actually are idiots (though you may be lucky) but because they have a thousand things going on in their lives and in the hyper connected world in which we live they may have a million things clamouring for their attention at any given moment. That means that you shouldn't expect them to be giving you 100% of their attention and analysing in detail everything you are saying. Nor should you expect them to have all the information that you have (or even the information you would imagine they *should* have). This is where awareness directors come into their own:
   > "Were you aware that..."
   > "If you permit me to draw your attention to the following key points"

"Perhaps no-one has told you that..."

"Maybe you were not informed about..." etc.

These are the verbal equivalents of highlighter pens. They can also serve to make your counterparts focus on some parts of your speech and not on others (equally important parts but perhaps you don't want them to give them too much attention).

B

21. **Back off:**

Give them time to think. If things have been intense and they have felt under pressure you can give them space to consider an offer. If you are not employing dirty tricks that you don't want them to discover (**hustle close** for example) this should do one or several of the following: reinforce trust between both sides; let them come with any questions or points of contention now, rather than after the deal has been signed; ensure that when they do sign, they do so feeling satisfied with the deal (meaning that the probability that they implement the deal as agreed is greater).

22. **Bad publicity:**

If you have access to the media, the company grapevine, or their mother and you also have even a whiff of wrongdoing on their part (real or invented, that depends on you, are you an Eagle or a Snake?) you can shame them into backing down on something or retracting a position. This can be especially useful and used positively if they are being a devil with you and want to maintain an image of being an angel with everyone else.

'Sure, you could ignore our demands and keep polluting the river. But then we could also go to the local television station and make sure that every time your workers go home their neighbours refuse to talk to them. But hey, that's your right. You are the big powerful company.

23. **Balanced Team:**
Rather than a trick or a tactic this is simply good business sense. It is not only to take advantage of the **Tag Team** ploy, but it is also so that you have different people who are experts on different subjects (marketing, finance etc.), or different skills (listening, questioning, analysing) or personalities (people-people, hard on the issues people, cautious-and-steady people, etc.). Bringing a balanced team (that works well together) is the equivalent of having a superman at the table.

24. **BATNA[2] baby!**
Deploy your BATNA or threaten to do so. You should have an alternative to this negotiation that you can walk away to if this negotiation fails. If they push you down too far let

---

[2] BATNA stands for Best Alternative To a Negotiated Agreement. It is what you have if you decide to get up and walk out of this negotiation. It is not the various alternatives you had before you entered the negotiation – some of them may have evaporated the moment you started this negotiation - or perhaps they improved the moment it got out that you were negotiating with someone else.

them know that you are quite happy to go with your other option (which could range from war to dealing with another supplier).

Be aware of the fact that their objective may simply be to find out what your best alternative is, so be careful about being too quick to expose your BATNA.

25. **Because**

Research has shown that even if you do not give a very convincing reason, that when you use the word 'because' for simple requests, there is a much greater probability that people will acquiesce than they would if the request is made on its own. Simple word, powerful effect.

The other effective use of 'because' is to ask the other negotiator to say why they have agreed to a certain proposal, or why they feel it would be good for them. When they preface their own answers with 'because' they also remember the proposal as more justified later on, and the fact that they were the ones saying 'because' makes it that much more convincing in their own mind.

26. **Big Body:**

Physical intimidation. When you are in a small room with a big person then you may feel pressured into accepting a deal, or not pushing for more, simply because a primal part of your brain says 'Be careful of this one, he's really big. And is that a scar running down his face? I'm sure that's a scar. Where the hell did he get that?'

27. **Big Car:**

    By driving up in a big/expensive car you convey power and success. Sometimes people will take you more seriously because they imagine that you know what you are talking about (On a psychological level there is an element of 'well, that's an expensive car, which means that he must be making a lot of money, which means he must be very good at what he is doing.') Little do they realise that the car has been rented for the day. Very few top level whizz kid consultants drive up in a people carrier and step out in an Armani suit. Variations of this are the helicopter ride and the private jet.

    The downsides of driving a flash car are obvious when you find yourself negotiating with Trade Unions about letting staff go ("he can drive a sports car but he can't pay for a few extra workers, well, we'll show him") or arguing with sales people that you can't pay more because your pockets are empty.

28. **Big Experience:**

    This plays on people's need to know that what you have done has already been tested somewhere else and works. It also establishes you as an expert in the field. This is not 'name dropping' on its own. This is pointing to success stories involving you, your department or your organisation. "When we carried out that project in Angola we did it like this."

"That's what we thought as well when we started that hotel in Shanghai and then we ran into these delays due to a shortage in Perspex wind vanes. I think we should calculate an overrun of at least two weeks to be on the safe side."

Testimonials from former clients also set up your 'Big Experience' much like a reference would on your C.V. 'Been there, done that' trumps theoretical ideas when employed correctly 'I know it looks good on paper but I remember when we were in Berlin and.....'.   Of course if you abuse this and constantly use 'Big Experience' as your only argument you will come across as a bore. If you are an older person this is the card to play over younger competitors.

'Sure, they look flashy and slick, but they don't know what they are doing. We have been around for twenty years and every problem you might encounter we have already solved. You should go with the tried and tested model.'

29. **Big favour, little favour**:
The trick here is to set up a round of giving and receiving where they end up giving after you. That very often means that what is given in return is bigger than what you initially gave them.   This is especially the case in some cultures where you can even get into a vicious circle of outdoing the other side's generosity (the exact opposite of clear headed negotiating in fact). Also see **reciprocity**.

30. **Big head-ing**:
    Confidence works in a negotiation. It has been shown that more confident people, people who are surer of their answers and opinions and more opinionated people are all considered more trustworthy than their wavering, doubting colleagues. Trust in a negotiation is like money in the bank. Anything that makes them trust you is good. However be careful of falling for '**massaging a big ego**' and having your bluff called.

31. **Big office:**
    This is the easiest way to intimidate the other side if they come to you (and for you to be intimidated if you represent a relatively smaller organisation and go to them). When you walk into a palatial office with views of the White House, enormous bay windows and a desk that is bigger than your first flat, it's hard not to be impressed. If people are territorial animals then an enormous office can send the signal that "this Lion has a big roar". I have been in companies where the person due to negotiate deliberately takes over the biggest office in the organisation for the duration of a negotiation with external clients. If you do this make sure that the photos on the desk do not have another person's family!

32. **Big Qualifications:**
    These can be on your business card (PhD, MBA etc.), on your CV, etc. and even better if they are from a prestigious

university. In some cultures and countries people are awed by titles. In other countries the more qualifications you have the less time you have actually spent in the real world working. Other people have all their qualifications (including that food handling cert they received when they were fifteen and working at the weekends in a fast food restaurant in their hometown) framed and hanging on the wall behind them where they are negotiating with you. The hope here is that you will be impressed by the image of the qualifications and not actually look closely. If you do you may wonder what university gives degrees in baking chestnuts and why that would be relevant to buying high tech equipment for the military. Of course it works better if it's a PhD from Stanford.

33. **Big reputation:**
'A good reputation is more valuable than money' said Publius Syrus over 2,000 years ago and things haven't changed much since then. If you go into a negotiation with a reputation for honesty and fairness that will help you a lot in the negotiation. If you have a reputation for being extremely hard then this can frighten the opposition before you even meet. If you have a reputation for being clever and smart then they may trust your calculations without taking them away to check themselves. If you have a reputation for being untrustworthy and backstabbing then be ready to pay extra for everything to compensate for the risk of doing business with you. Think about what you have a reputation for. If it suits you then cultivate it and protect

it. If you do not take care of it remember that one good act doesn't make an angel out of a devil but one bad act sends an angel tumbling from heaven.

34. **Big title:**
Vice-president of Sales, Mid-West Region. Sounds good. Director of Finance, Central Division. Can you smell the power? Titles - get them and use them. If the other side considers you to be a person with authority within your own organisation there is a strong chance they will take you more seriously. Of course, the people at the top of the company generally don't have to throw their titles around, because everyone knows who they are.

The expression 'the pecking order' comes from the world of chickens. In every chicken coop there is a top hen that can peck all the other hens and no other hen can peck her. Below that hen there is a hen that only the top hen can peck and no-one else can peck. That goes all the way down to the poor hen at the bottom that all the hens can peck and isn't allowed to peck any other hen. You can recognise that miserable hen as the one missing all the feathers. When you are negotiating you do not want to come across as that particular hen in your company or your negotiating counterparts will start to peck you as well.

However when you are negotiating with other companies be careful of being taken in by their impressive sounding titles. In some small companies everyone is a director of something and there are banks where every second person is a vice-president of this or that.

35. **Big dresser:**

Expensive suit, gold Swiss watch, diamond cufflinks, patent leather shoes. When you walk in the door you will exude power. In an ideal world people should look to the heart of a man or woman, but in this world so many people never get past the clothes. Dress with style - people treat you better. (See **Halo Effect**). You may also feel more confident as a result (even if the other person cannot immediately recognise the quality of the clothes you wear.) From the moment the first cave man decided to put a little circle on his head and call himself 'Chief', people have looked at the accessories we wear to give them clues as to our power status. Of course, as mentioned with **Big Car**, don't try to argue that you have zero money in your account when you are wearing a diamond necklace.

36. **Blackmail:**

This is the ultimate leverage, and you have to be particularly unscrupulous to use it. However when it comes to negotiating there seem to be many unscrupulous people out there. You go drinking with them in a foreign country and commit a sexual transgression. The next day those hints that your spouse would be very interested in what you had got up to may well mean that you will be softer on them to keep them on side. You might even close a deal that in other situations you would turn down.

Another case could be where you accept the equivalent of a bribe ("hey, it's the way they do business here") and then find that you have trapped yourself (if the business deal goes south and your company/the police find out about what you have done, who gets stung the worst – you or the company that gave you the bribe? Answer, you don't care, YOU will get stung and you don't give a damn what happens to them!). Or else it could be more elaborate and you could be set up by the other side and the blackmail special pack comes complete with photos, videos and the actual hand cuffs you were wearing.

37. **Blind with science/numbers:**

It is amazing how many times people do not question the 'facts' they are presented with (especially if they consider you an expert on a subject). Oftentimes they do not even listen carefully to the details. I have listened to so many news reports where the anchor in the studio gives a figure of '100,000 people left homeless by the floods' and the reporter on the ground immediately afterwards starts with 'Here we are in Marajinpoor where 150,000 people have been left without a home.' No-one seems to care that the figure has been inflated by 50%.

Of course when it comes to the actual haggling and writing up of contracts everyone pays attention. But when you are putting forward your arguments at the beginning rarely is a throwaway phrase such as '20% of our customers preferred this option because they felt the extra expense was worth the security it gave them' questioned when you have established trust.

Surveys have shown that people prefer milk that is 99% fat free as opposed to milk that is 1% fat. What is more surprizing is that subsequent surveys showed that people preferred milk that was 98% fat free to milk that was 1% fat. People actually prefer more fat when the numbers are dressed up!

Sometimes we don't even listen to the numbers themselves but we are influenced by the person who seemingly wields them with panache. Lesson? You should be careful if you use this tactic (all you need is one person who knows what you're talking about to torpedo your credibility if you are lying) but remember that it *is* widely used because it's effective.   Some people even base a political career on it! Listen carefully to what they are saying and ask yourself whether it is relevant or not to the negotiation. If it is indeed relevant then check to see if it is true (and remember, relevant can mean something as simple as establishing their authority)

38. **Blowfish**:

Showing that you are confident when you have nothing inside but hot air. There are people who will convince you of their arguments simply because they come across as extremely confident. It has been shown that a doctor who checks with a colleague or looks something up in a medical dictionary before confirming your diagnosis is seen as less competent than the one who confidently tells you what is wrong with you without consulting anyone or anything. We mistake confidence for knowledge. Sadly confident people are sometimes con artists and sometimes they know so little about a subject that they don't know they could be wrong. Beware of confidence in others but as a general rule make sure that you arm yourself with it. See **Big Heading, Bluff.**

39. **Bluff**:

    Good luck here. Some people can do it and some people can't. Pretend you have a stronger hand than you really do. Especially important for combining with **poker face, big head-ing** and **shock openings**. If you can't control your body language then don't even bother trying this or your **ethos** will go straight out the window. In the broadest sense of the word it is used by man negotiators to some degree to cover up their weaknesses.

40. **Body language:**

    There are lots of statistics out there that give figures like 7% of what we communicate is with words, 38% with intonation and a massive 65% with body language. Of course these statistics are not entirely correct(try guessing someone's phone number just by looking at their body language and you will realise that verbal communication is pretty important) but they do give an indication that body language is extremely important. If you are shoving my head under water while snarling 'I love you', I'll probably go with the body language.

In a negotiation huge amounts of communication are carried out by your body and not by your mouth. Arms suddenly crossed and leaning back indicate rejection, rubbing your nose is interpreted as nervous or lying, suddenly opening your eyes indicate your surprize at a proposal (which can be nicely followed up by crossed arms and sitting back in your chair) etc. You cannot rely 100% on body language cues (you could follow them up with 'I sense you are....' to confirm your intuition.) but you would be a fool to ignore them completely.

It can help to have someone observing the other side while you talk. If you detect that the other person is nervous, or feel they are lying about a certain point then it might be worth pushing them on this area. Likewise you should be aware of the signals your own body is sending. You may have to learn to tone down your gestures if you use your hands a lot but don't then overcompensate for their quietness by turning your eyebrows into a pair of dancing caterpillars that give everything away. Your counterpart may, even at a subconscious level, not trust what you are saying because of *your* body language.

41. **Bracketing**:

The other side has stated their number first – let's say $20. The person who decides the final settlement point is very often the person who 'brackets' that figure. For example, if you come back with $30 then the middle point (where the negotiation tends to gravitate towards) will be $25. However if you come back with $100 then the middle point will be $60. The person who brackets (makes their offer second) has a lot of power when you have reached the haggling point of the negotiation. This may not be as useful when there is price transparency or you know less about the price than they do and by making your offer second you are reacting to their anchor (see **anchoring**).

42. **Brainstorm**:

Creativity is your ally in a negotiation. Normally conflict is created because people are looking at the problem in the frame that has been given them (namely *we* want to increase/decrease price (or claim this piece of land) and *they* want to do the opposite).

If you practice creativity (good news – everyone is creative, but many of us don't exercise that part of our brain very often) or even set aside a part of your team meetings to finding alternative ideas then you will find yourself coming up with solutions to apparent impasses. In these sessions it is important to set parameters for your creativity and a time limit. Then within that there can be no judgements or dampening of other people's ideas. What might seem crazy to you could be the catalyst for someone else to go off on a very constructive tangent. However if you start being critical at this stage of the process then people will be reluctant to come forward with new ideas. If you practice brainstorming then there is also a greater chance that you will be able to **increase the size of the pie.**

43. **Bribery**:

    Setting aside the ethics of giving and receiving bribes for the moment let's accept the fact that this practice happens in many industries and in many countries around the world. In some places it is considered standard practice, in others it is considered illegal (but relatively common). You pay for a favour and you get the deal. The person you are bribing gets an amount that is a lot for them but relatively little when the entire value of the deal is taken into account. Bribes can take many forms apart from an envelope/suit case/small truck full of cash. It might be 'if you give me this deal, I will make sure your brother's company is subcontracted to do the construction work on the plant.' It is no good simply stating that you do not accept or give bribes. You have to take into account how this will affect your business and then plan accordingly (for example, I will not give a bribe but I will plan to call a public enquiry into the local government giving a contract to the most expensive supplier in the public auction.)

44. **Bring a friend:**

    You might be completely competent to negotiate on your own. You might be an expert in the field, with years of experience. However, having someone who can listen to the other side while you talk, who can back up your arguments, who can give you support in breaks, who can take over for you when you need to sit back and rest etc.

rarely hurts. If you are a small company you may not feel like the extra expense. If you are in a conflict negotiation you may feel that you do not want to intimidate the other side. However, you should balance the pros and cons and give serious consideration to *"bringing a friend"*.

45. **Brinkmanship**:

The negotiations go right to the edge, to the final deadline, to the point of violence, deadlock or breaking the deal. Both sides will lose if the deal doesn't happen. Some people crack under the pressure and make concessions. Others do not. Some people can do this, others can't. If you can then you gain a great advantage over the other side, unless you are both experts at playing 'chicken' and the negotiation ends up crashing into a wall. Many people crack under the pressure of going to the brink and make concessions just to pull back. This is a risky game to play and takes on many forms (pretending you're not interested, using silence, encouraging deadlocks, making excessive demands and then shutting up etc.) but the reason people as famous as Henry Kissinger have done and continue to do it is because it can pay great dividends. Ask yourself if you work well under pressure, if you are able to keep a poker face and if you reasonably feel that the other side could give in on whatever you are asking. If the answer to all of these is yes then good luck!

46. **Brooklyn optician:**

You see a sign in an optician 'Glasses, $15" and you think: "that's a great offer, I'll go in." You sit down and get your eyes tested for free (gaining a commitment of time from you, and giving you something for 'free' that you will feel somewhat obliged to repay) and then they bring out the $15 dollar glasses. The spectacles are not, shall we say, the most attractive in the world. You see social exclusion and nights spent alone in the corners of cocktail parties looming ahead of you. To get the nicer looking frame you will have to pay $90. Ok you say. Then it's $30 dollars for the lenses. Ok. For each lens. Ok. Plus the anti-glare coating, $20 dollars. Ok. Each. Ok. Plus the 2 year breakages guarantee (a must as your glasses are now so expensive). Ok. And the list goes on and on until you finally gasp 'Stop!' knowing that you will have to re-mortgage your house to pay for a pair of special offer spectacles. The Brooklyn optician adds and adds bit by bit from whatever offer originally grabbed your attention so the final deal is no-where near what you originally planned. They will keep adding while you let them.

47. **Buy Time to Think:**

Some people handle pressure very well and think clearly regardless of the situation. However for many mere mortals a negotiation in a high pressure situation results in thinking processes getting muddled and slowing down. If that is your case then you have to buy time to think. Phone calls to the home office, call for caucus, or a few moments to study a document that you already understand are all useful for creating a bit of space for you to think about the negotiation so far.

48. **By-the-way:**

"Nice conversation, nice conversation, nice conversation. Blah, blah, blah. We're all friends. Lovely weather we're having. By-the-way, you're fired." In a negotiation this can be a very easy way to introduce an idea, inoffensively and in an offhand manner, even though it is the main issue you want. This phrase makes it look as if the issue is not that important to you and is just a throw away request. The result is that the other side may give it to you without even asking for anything in return.

'We'd like the car in red. By-the-way, how about throwing in the insurance for free?'

C

---

49. **Calendar close:**

Don't simply leave the meeting on a good note and accept a promise that they'll get back in touch with you to settle details ....at some stage in the future. Put the date in your diary and get them to put it in theirs. You agree a date that a decision will be taken, that the contract will be formally signed, the product delivered or the service rendered. When you leave without a calendar close, life has a tendency to get in the way of good intentions and the hot feelings they had in the negotiation gradually cool. Plan for that NOT to happen.

50. **Call a friend:**

If there is a third party (or third parties) that could shift the balance of power you can always offer to 'call them, I think have them on speed dial' to come in and offer to mediate, or to help your negotiating counterpart make up their mind. This can be a veiled threat or a show of power. If you are lucky they never force you to make the call and you don't end up owing your 'friend' a favour.

51. **Call in the cavalry:**

    At a key moment in the negotiation you bring in your boss to help you with the negotiations. If they are senior to the other side their presence can intimidate and lend psychological power to your side. You can also use them to break a deadlock by making a concession on a specific issue that you couldn't make, up until then (without you losing face by backing down – possible if you had already established the limits of your authority up to that concession point). Or else their presence can indicate that a concession is genuine and will not be whittled down later. Or in many case they can act as the bad cop to your good cop. When their job is done they should leave because if they don't there's not much sense in you being there. They should also have a good excuse for not being there all the time.   For example saying "Excuse me, I have to go the bathroom again, bladder like a kitten sitting beside a fountain' will probably not cut it.

52. **Call the mother-in-law:**

    This tactic is the equivalent in a domestic argument of calling the mother-in-law, arguing your case with them, and then getting them to speak to your spouse. I would not necessarily advise this as a good tactic in marriage but in a negotiation it may be necessary. It specifically means speaking to someone on their side, definitely not neutral, who is prepared to listen and will speak/communicate/negotiate with your real counterpart for you. This may be necessary when emotions are running high or where your counterpart is obviously unaware of the benefits available to them. To be deployed in a conflict setting as opposed to simply selling them a car.

53. **Cards on the table:**
This could be a genuine call for honesty and an open exploration of interests to find common points and try to reach a mutually beneficial solution, or not. One side may put their cards on the table while the other side resolutely keeps their cards up their sleeve. Guess which one suggested to 'put our cards on the table'?

54. **Cash cows:**
Don't think that a short term big-win is better than a long term repeat small win. Your bread and butter generally come from the Cash Cows, those regular clients that pay often and reliably. Being a Cash Cow for the other negotiator gives you leverage when negotiating with them and enables you to demand concessions, respect, and a nicer holiday card.

55. **Change the goal posts:**
In a negotiation you better make sure that you have clearly defined, and agreed on what the other side wants. If not, as soon as you reach what you think is an agreement (by making substantial concessions from your side) they

suddenly move the goal posts and say that they didn't actually want what you thought they did (though they don't give back the concessions you have made). They can do this indefinitely until you finally do decide to get a firm clarification of their objectives for the negotiation. You should then add 'nothing is negotiated until everything is negotiated' and make all offers from your side conditional and temporary.

56. **Changing seats at the table:**

Sometimes you can change the entire dynamics of the negotiation by simply getting up and walking around to the other side of the table and sitting down beside them (you may not want to be too dramatic about this or you could scare the hell out of them, especially if you have been **Big Body**ing up until then.) Suddenly you are no longer opponents staring each other down, but two people looking at a common problem together, minus the barriers.

57. **Changing the standards:**

Be careful if they do this to you as it is akin to changing the goal posts. It happens typically with banks ("I'm afraid that was the standard interest rate for last month"). Watch out for this because changing the standards in one area should change the whole package and you should argue for that. From your side you may wish to change the standards being used in the negotiation if you feel that the ones that are set by the other side are biased, outdated or simply not relevant. Do not feel that you have to accept the default standards just because they are standard! Every negotiation is different. So in summary: do not let them do it, but if you do then it's fine.

58. **Cherry picking:**

This is the classic negotiating ploy. Choose the best elements of several different offers from various competitors/packages and then group them together into the ideal package. You put forward this hypothetical package as the one to beat when dealing with a seller in order to improve what you are being offered by the people you are currently dealing with. If they know what they are doing, and the market, then they will point out that no vendor is offering that 'dream' package.

59. **Circumstances have changed:**

Arguing that you don't have to accept the agreement as originally stipulated because the circumstances that made the original agreement possible are no longer the same. If they want to continue doing business with you they will have to accept the new reality. See **Hot Potato** and **"It's a deal... let's negotiate**". This can, like many of the tactics in this book, be done in good faith or bad. You will have to take a decision to be flexible or not depending on the context (your need to keep this client, trust etc.)

60. **Coalitions**:

In a multiparty negotiation ten small parties working well together can beat one large party (all you have to do is look at the politics of the European Union). Studies have also shown that the coalition that reaches a critical mass first has a serious advantage in any negotiation. In any multiparty negotiation remember you are not an island: That means buttering up others before you reach the negotiation table and accepting that you will have to make concessions to your own side as well as to the other.

61. **Coercion**:

Technically the moment you force the other side to do something it stops being a negotiation (as we define negotiations as something voluntarily entered into). However if you understand coercion to read 'extreme pressure' then this is another type of power in your arsenal. It could involve **threats, force projection, punish power, blackmail, intimidation** etc. Remember that many people will not forgive you once you start to use coercion and the moment they can turn the tables they will (and even if they cannot turn the tables they will look for ways to get out of the deal with you). However, as Keynes says, in the 'long run we're all dead' so many negotiators happily use coercion as standard practice. Why? It works. It is why in an unfair world bullies often get their own way.

62. **Comparing:**

   If you have two products people can choose independently between them, and very often they will choose the cheaper option. However if you introduce a similar, but much more expensive, product to the more costly of the original two products then there is a dramatic shift towards purchasing what is now the 'middle' option.

   When people compare now, they almost ignore the cheaper model altogether and begin to compare the two similar, top-end, items and then choose the one which is obviously of greater value for money.

63. **Compromise**:

   The simplest way of negotiating. Similar to '**split the difference'** but it might be both of you giving in on totally different issues ("we'll take off the no-breakages policy if you agree to pay for part of the marketing"). Make sure that your compromises are equal (i.e. you both make concessions, not just a one way street) and preferably **conditional** (see below)

64. **Commitment traps**:

   If you can get the other side to commit to different points you can use these commitments to trap them later. Typically used as:

   "Do want to save money?"

   Yes

"After everything I have told you can you see how this product/service can save you money?"
Yes.
"When would you like to start saving money?"
Now.
"Don't you think you should buy this product/service now?"
By question three the knot is already starting to tighten as they have found themselves trapped by their own answers. They can now show themselves to be consistent people and fall on their swords or prove to the world that they are dreaded flip-floppers and back away from what they have already said! Commitment traps can also be used effectively to stop people reneging on agreements. See **magic writing.**

65. **Commitment ploy**:
You announce to the general public, the media, important neutral parties or in a formal declaration at the beginning of the negotiation that you are not going to budge a single inch on points A, B, or C. You have committed yourself publicly to this and if you back down you will lose face. This does not mean you will not back down. It does mean that you will want something tasty and substantial in return for that loss of face. Commitment ploys can be risky because they introduce a level of inflexibility into the negotiation that rarely helps. They can be very popular with your home constituents for which these ploys are very often intended. Commonly combined with **stonewalling.**

66. **Conceal:**

To a greater or lesser extent this is a strategy employed by most negotiators (except a Penguin). You have to decide beforehand what you are going to conceal, and for how long. An Eagle negotiator might go so far as to reveal all of his/her interests but conceal their alternatives, or lack thereof. A Chimpanzee would conceal their objectives, their interests, their real requests, their weaknesses, their real strengths and perhaps even the location of the nearest bathroom!

Concealing can go from simply knowing when to keep your mouth shut to outright lying. What level of concealment you choose has to match your own moral compass - but it is a good idea to take that decision before the negotiation, and not during it, and to make all team members aware of it so later there are no accusations of 'I can't believe you told them X!'

67. **Concession Close:**

The very simple technique of asking them if they would be prepare to sign the contract *now*, agree to the deal *now*, or shake hands on the agreement *now*, if you were prepared to give in on X issue. The deal may be completely biased in your favour but if they feel they are going to get that concession at the end you can very often close on that positive feeling. See **Last Concession Lost.**

68. **Conditional concessions:**

Everything you give is conditional on getting something in exchange. You can start with the "second conditional" to test waters:

"If you gave (past tense) us that then we would give (conditional) this."

When you are being more direct and definite you can use the first conditional:

"If you give us (present) that then we will give (you) this."

You will notice that in both cases whatever you offer them is conditional on *first* receiving what they have:

"I will give you this *only* if you give me that first."

69. **Confidence:**

When this is natural, it's good. You come across as more convincing, more trustworthy, and with greater authority. When you are acting it starts to slip into **big head-ing.**

70. **Confirmation bias:**

Build on your reputation using confirmation bias (and be careful of falling into the same trap). When people have a certain image/opinion of you they will only see the side of what you say and do that supports that previous image/opinion and will filter everything else out. If you have a fair idea of what they think of you then you can use that to your advantage. If they think you are stupid (and that suits your strategy) then you can be as smart as you want and disguise it as accidents and good luck. They will perceive your actions that way as it matches up with their image of you being stupid, and will not suspect that they are being conned.   If they do realise their mistake, it's generally too late. Confirmation bias can also work with you/against you if they like/dislike you when the negotiation starts.

71. **Consult with the pillow:**

Sleeping on an issue helps in many ways. You can come up with a creative solution to a thorny problem. You can let emotions cool and take a more rational decision (devoid of arousal, pity or anger). The distance of a day sometimes is enough to see the bigger picture clearly. Even better if you have an entire weekend before you sign the contract.

72. **Contrast Principle:**

Don't just reach an agreement - remind them of what you were asking for at the beginning and tell them how far you've come down now to reach this deal. Contrast what they have with what you had offered so they realise what a good deal they have (as opposed to simply focusing on the haggling of the last 10% of the negotiation). That way you will limit the possibilities of the **winner's frown** on their side and any desire on their part to do even better in the next round of negotiations with you.

73. **Control Expectations**:

It is normal for both sides to go in with excessive demands that have no way of being satisfied in the negotiation. A large part of your negotiating skills may simply be used up on explaining to the other side the reality of the situation i.e. they are not going to get what they are looking for and they better get used to the idea fairly fast or the negotiation is going nowhere. Combine **awareness directors, "We'd love to but...", softeners** and **objective standards** (and possibly "**you've got to be kidding**") to bring them down to earth.

74. **Controlling the agenda:**

There is huge power in controlling the agenda. To the extent that at a lot of top level meetings there are pre-negotiations simply to decide what will be on the agenda. If it is not on the agenda then it is not discussed (or it can be very difficult to get it on the agenda later) and if it is not discussed then it doesn't matter what your opinion is, you are not going to get anywhere with it. Always bring your own agenda if that role has not been formally assigned. Chances are that if you are the only side that brings an agenda you can control the flow of the meeting. They may make changes and adjustments but they are doing using your agenda as a base/template. If you both have agendas then you can find a compromise between both of them – without having to blindly accept theirs (unless they accept that you are making a conditional concession and you offer to draw up the contract afterwards in exchange).

75. **COTS**:

    Cash **o**n **t**he **s**pot. You gain an advantage if you can pay cash immediately. You can ask for a lower price, compete better against those who require payment terms and there is the power of confidence when you are able to pay whatever price you have agreed in hard currency. Dangers? If they get the cash then it can be difficult to get it back after service/product has been delivered. Hence the fact that they have to give you a better deal to accept the risk.

76. **Covert Intimidation:**

    Letting them work against themselves. They feel bad mentally and physically because of their surroundings and as a result they start to reduce their own expectations, all without you having to say anything. See **Open Door, Big office, Big dresser, Fatigue, Hunger, Keeping you waiting, light in your eyes, location, small chairs and tall tables, squashed at a table.** The combination of all these and perhaps even seeing your main competitor shake hands with the buyer just before you walk in, can all add up to intimidate you (with your own brain doing the intimidating)

77. **Crazy power:**

    If people are not sure how you are going to act or respond (will they storm out, shoot me or laugh?) then they are more cautious when dealing with you. They are more moderate in their demands and use fewer aggravators when speaking to you. Just imagine negotiating with a drug addict who has your husband or wife hostage. They ask for $100,000. You probably won't laugh in their face and tell them "$20 dollars, take it or leave it" (unless you are going through a particularly bad moment with your spouse). In hostage negotiations this sometimes means that a more aggressive approach to the situation is taken (S.W.A.T. team for example) if it is felt that the person has too much crazy power and an alternative to negotiating is required.

78. **Crocodile tears:**

Some people crumble when they are faced with another person crying. Your initially tough stance and demands for more concessions now just seem cruel and unnecessary. If you are the person who has the power to take the decision then it can be very difficult to resist. Some people are absolutely fantastic at turning on the water works when necessary. If you have a **higher authority** this can help you to protect your demands while being sympathetic with the person in front of you. How many bank managers have the power to take your money but have to consult with the head office before they make any concessions? They come across as very mean when faced with a little old widow who is crying, but this policy does protect the bank manager from the unscrupulous actor who is trying to get a better deal. As they say in Spanish 'The innocents pay for the sinners'.

79. **Cry innocent:**
Make mistakes and then put on an innocent expression "what me? Con you? Never. Come on, we're friends." Use this with **Hurt and Betrayed, Deliberate Mistake, Crocodile Tears, Playing Dumb**. If you have a good relationship it may work, if you do not then it will probably strain it further.

80. **Cry me a river (of gold):**
Research shows that people who are sad make worse negotiation decisions. Sellers accept less for what they are selling and buyers pay up to 30% more for what they are getting when feelings of sadness have been induced in them. If you are an unscrupulous negotiator you may want to investigate how to make them feel sad just before you start haggling. However, for everyone else the important thing to remember is that you should be aware of your mood and how it may affect your negotiation, and perhaps wait until you are feeling happier before you start horse trading.

81. **Culture A – "that's the way we do things round here".**
"I'd love to help you but I'm afraid it's company policy."
"That might be how they do things in Moscow, but here in St. Petersburg we do things a little differently."
Culture (company or national) can be blamed for many things, but mainly it's a handy excuse for not making any

concessions or changes that would suit the other party. It is so general that it is difficult to argue with.

82. **Culture B - what you're saying/asking for is offensive here.**

A play on the previous point but this time you are taking it to the next level.

'We couldn't possibly do that. We'd be destroyed in the press/by our families/by the trade unions. We'd love to help you but I'm afraid there's just no way I could present that to my people.'

83. **Culture C – Forgive me and let me keep on doing it.**

You can be as direct as you want if it suits your needs and then apologise and say your culture is very direct (and then continue being so). You can avoid drinking late into the evening and being destroyed the next day. You can avoid drinking at lunch and keep a clear head. Put it all down to your home culture (unless you are famous for coming from a hard drinking culture!). This is useful for excusing rude behaviour, excessive hospitality, delays, vague language, anything you want in fact as long as you are dealing with people from another culture.

D

84. **Deadlines**:

Push someone up against a wall and they will take a decision quickly. Give them all the time in the world and they may never take a decision. Connect this with the **calendar close** if you want to avoid ending up waiting and waiting with nothing to show for it.. You can also give them a certain length of time to reach a deal or there will be no deal. The fact that there are so many 11th hour deals shows how effectively deadlines work in reality. See **80/20** and **Time Pressure Cooker** and **false deadlines.**

85. **Deadlock**:

If you're comfortable with them then by all means encourage them as part of your strategy (though selectively or the negotiation just bogs down with no forward movement and the other side may just decide to give up from exhaustion).The other side will make the concession to get out of them. True deadlocks rarely exist (and if one does and you have to abandon the deal, then it's not the end of the world. Remember, no deal is better than a bad deal) See **Brinkmanship** and **Stonewalling**.

86. **Decoy**:
Distract them with side issues that are less important and then whack them with a **by-the-way**. Decoys can also help you waste time if you're trying to push them against their deadlines.

87. **Decrease issues**:
Sometimes you cannot get anywhere because there are too many issues on the table. You might have to reduce the issues down to a more manageable number for this particular negotiation or engage in **phasing** so that you can deal with the issues in groups. This is much easier if you control the agenda.

88. **Deep pockets:**
Economic power. You deploy your resources to show very quickly that you can outlast them, out lawyer them, out buy them etc. and they would be better off not putting up a fight (or even think about tricking you). You should do this early and strong if you are going to use it as a tactic. It is not the same as **coercive power** (it simply shows you have massive **reward** and **punish power**)

89. **Defensive-offence**:

    This is the technique of starting with an attack on your product/service and then coming back with your argument. "Some people say to me "*objection/problem*" but I know that...." You know what they are going to say (because everyone does) but you already have your counter prepared. The danger of this tactic of course is that you make them focus on whatever you are defending as opposed to looking at the solution you are offering. Only do this if you are convinced they are going to come out with the objection.

    > "Some people say to me that there is no-way you can get so much mileage from so little but I have driven one of these models myself for years and I can tell you it's true. Others say to me that there is no way we could use this as a family car but I know a friend who has three children and a dog and they go on holidays to the beach every year with this car."

90. **Delaying ploy:**

    This can go anywhere from stepping out to go to the toilet to arranging and cancelling meetings for several months. Why would you do this? Well it depends on your objectives. It could be to buy time to think. It could be to buy time to investigate other options, or to build up your BATNA (see **BATNA baby!**), or to weaken theirs, or to get enough power/money to improve your bargaining position, or in the hope that the other side will give up and get the blame for scuppering the negotiations, or it might just be in order to wait until the macro-situation is ripe for a negotiation to take place with some hope for success.

91. **Deliberate error:**
This happens at the stage of signing the contract. Everything has been agreed and one side draws up the contract. Mistakes are made in the contract, percentages are increased by slight margins etc. If the other side notices then you **cry innocent** and pretend that they were mistakes. You can then add insult to injury and brush the changes off as so minor that there is no point in drawing up another contract. Of course, if the other side doesn't notice the changes before they sign then all the better. This is considered unethical by every negotiator I have ever met. And yet everyone I know who negotiates regularly has suffered this tactic at least once. Read every contract carefully and even better **write the contract** yourself.

92. **Differentiate or Die:**
Some people say this is dead in a world where everything is about cost and price. If you do decide to compete on price then your point of differentiation better be the most cost efficient operation in the business. If this is not the case and you do not have a clear means of reducing costs more than your competitors then competing with price is a race to the bottom that can burn everyone out.
Identify what makes you different and in the negotiation this should be part of your arguments and your proposal, to

avoid it turning into a black and white price negotiation. .
See **Unique.**

93. **Disinterest:**

    Like a cat strutting past you as if you are worth nothing this
    is a tactic used to a greater or lesser degree by the vast
    majority of negotiators. Unless you are a professional at
    this who is able to get people begging to do business with
    them (or at least look their way) be careful of showing so
    much disinterest that they are insulted or feel that there is
    no point in doing any business with you. .

94. **Distract and sign:**

    Con artists do this all the time – using cognitive overload to
    their advantage. You are given something to sign (like a
    contract) and then they ask you questions and talk to you
    about your family so you end up skimming the document
    instead of reading it properly. If this is done to you there is
    a greater chance of you not picking up on **deliberate
    errors**. This distraction might also be them spilling some
    coffee on the other side of the table and making a drama of
    cleaning it up or talking loudly with your colleagues or with
    their own.   Remember: distractions and contracts do not
    make good companions.

95. **Divide and conquer:**

    Identify differences on the other side and exploit them. By
    offering a threat and a short term reward in the same

proposal some people will respond to the threat and others to the reward. If you have noticed that some people on the team are quite greedy/impatient, and others are terrified of the consequences of no deal then you can set up a scenario where they argue among themselves. The greedy/impatient ones will go for the short term reward and the frightened ones will not want to risk the deal not going through. Both will go against the clear headed, hardnosed negotiators on their own side. Result: They will start fighting among themselves. Even if the more steely hearted ones win out they will know that they cannot push things too far/hard or they will risk another revolt from their own side.

96. Don't take no for an answer:

A simple 'no' is not an answer. In the world outside negotiations 'no means no' and you don't have to give any explanations and you are not entitled to demand any. However in a negotiation you should never simply accept 'no'. You must do your best to find out why. Is their opposition due to the proposal, the timing, the presentation, one particular part of it, what? 'No' on its own doesn't tell you anything.

97. Double agent:

Someone on their side who is working for you. Like finding the mother lode. More common than you might think. Someone on the Trade Union side who is secretly working for the managers. Someone on your team who is hoping to go and work in future with your competitors. They may simply destroy your side's position from the inside or give over all information to your opponents. If you feel that this is happening then you should drag out the negotiations and spend time identifying who that person is. Otherwise suspicions and mistrust will break up your team. Lethal when combined with **Divide and Conquer**.

98. **Double bind:**

"Do you want that in red or in blue?" "Do you want that tomorrow or next Monday?" This is very similar to the **assumptive close**. The Double Bind is used by hypnotists to give the **appearance of choice** but really you have none as you are being locked into doing something the other person wants if you answer red or blue, tomorrow or Monday. Be very careful of these Double Binds and be ready to say 'neither in fact' or simply 'we haven't taken any decision yet, but we'll let you know.'

E

99. **Ego trap:**

"So you're the boss then, eh? You take all the decisions, do you? No-one tells you how to run your company/house, eh?" Cue maniacal laughter and rubbing hands together in glee. If you have been established as the expert on a subject, the top boss or the *real* decision maker then it can be very difficult for you to retreat from your statements without a loss of ego. 'Well, if you are the boss then is there any reason why you can't take a decision on this today if you like it?' Equally effective when you find ego maniacs that you can use it on.

100. **Email:**

It has been shown in recent experiments that people with less power are better off negotiating virtually (by email) instead of face to face. When you have less power you feel weaker in the face-to-face negotiation which means you give away even more than you have to. When you are not in the same room as the other person and don't have to see them you can eliminate feelings of inferiority and the racing heart that will drive your expectations even lower. So if you feel you are in a much weaker position then try and go for the virtual option.

101. **Embedded commands**:

"I'd like you to (*tiny pause*) sign this contract." "Perhaps you could (*tiny pause*) think about this proposal and see where it meets your needs." People react badly to imperative statements when they are aware of them (hark back to when you were thirteen – "no-one tells me to tidy my bedroom!") but respond almost automatically when they are not. That tiny pause innocuously separates the request part of the phrase from the command so you can say it in a way that is effective without causing offense. So, I'd like you to... remember embedded commands and use them in your negotiations.

102. **Empty pockets:**

This is a regular ploy on the buyer's side. They are interested, but they just don't have the cash for whatever you are offering. Do not make the mistake of automatically reducing the price to match the level of money in their pockets. Find out when they *will* have money, find out if there are any features of your product or service that you can slice off to bring the price down. I repeat: avoid unilateral price drops in response to Empty pockets.

103. **Empty promises**:

The most common of the dirty tricks. Promise everything until you have to sign the contract. Get them negotiating, get them interested, get them signing with whatever promise you have to make. Then withdraw the promises or assure them that even though they are not in the contract they will be implemented. Contract signed, money in the bank, "Oh, sorry, did we promise that? There's no way we can do that. Was that the sales person who told you that? Oh, they've left the company now. I'm afraid. No, I'm sorry, there's no refund, *that* is in the contract." See **9/10s of the law**.

104. **Escalation**:

This can be done the nice way or the nasty way. The nasty way is where you reach the end of the negotiation, feel that the agreement is about to be signed and the other side comes along, scraps the deal and asks for a lot more (or wants to pay a lot less) i.e. escalates.

The nice way to escalate is at the beginning of the negotiation where you revise what the other side felt was the initial bargaining position by asking for a lot more/less than they proposed (which was an initially extreme offer to start off with).   They then talk you down/up to a reasonable middle point and you both feel that you have won in the negotiation.

105. **Establish the rules of the game:**

This does not mean the agenda. This means who gets to speak, and when, and how. Turn taking, language used, breaks, the process itself. All of these are the rules of the game. If you take charge of the rules of the game (you don't have to be aggressive about it, you can just as easily suggest what you feel would be sensible ground rules to make the negotiation go smoother.). If they play by the rules you have put forward then you are at an advantage (even if they would have suggested the same ones) because psychologically you have shown that you are in charge.

106. **Ethos:**

This translates loosely as credibility and authority, one of Aristotle's three requirements for artistic persuasion (the Maoris call it *mana*). Do you have credibility and authority that you can leverage to persuade the other side? If not, what can you do to get it? They may even see you as the enemy and still be credible. Ethos does not have to be something you get from your friends. Your friends may not even give it to you. However if you have zero ethos with your counterpart then you will find the going tough every time you have to try and persuade them.

107. **Exceptions:**

Sometimes the other side will take the entire deal apart in the exceptions that are inserted into the contract. "We will pay you the full amount except when it is the weekend, or a day when we are working, or on a day when the sun rises, or on every odd day, or even." Treat the exceptions with great care and negotiate them as carefully as you would any other issue in the negotiation (they are often inserted using the **Quivering Quill** technique)

108. **Experience shows that…:**

This is a powerful sentence as it implies that *you* have experience in this area without actually saying it. If you are called up on this then you can bring out the references and sources who *have* had this experience. If you can carry it off with confidence then you won't be questioned. Used effectively you can gain the advantage of being considered an expert without worrying as much about falling into the trap of **Ego**. A similar example of this in use is 'studies have shown' without ever referencing the studies.

109. **Expert:**

See **Third party Experts**, or **Bring a friend**, or **Big Experience/Qualifications** if *you* are the Expert. This may give you greater authority, credibility and trust and if you are dealing with inexperienced or weaker negotiators then this gives you even greater power. As always, be careful of being trapped by the label of Expert - if they prove that you are wrong on any point it will affect your credibility disproportionately and they may also use it against you 'well, as you know, this is the standard rate in the industry for that service' (if you do not know it is the standard rate then what do you do? Hand the mantle of expert to them or go with it?)

110. **Explain to me why...:**

People often react defensively to a direct 'Why are you doing that?' However, when you put it in the sentence 'Explain to me why...' you come across as more empathetic, less accusing and more interested. Result: more information for you. More information for you = more power. Variations would be 'How did you come to that decision?' and 'What led you to believe that?'

F

---

111. **Fair**:

'I think that's a fair offer.' 'Let's be fair.' 'This is a fair deal.' 'We're going to have to be fair to everyone concerned'. If you're lucky no-one will actually question what 'fair' means. People want fairness in a deal, or at least the appearance of it. It has been shown that even monkeys want it and would prefer to go hungry rather than accept an unfair situation.

Fair is a common word to bandy around in negotiations and is much abused. Saying something is fair if you genuinely mean it is fine but very often it's just a quick solution/phrase that only suits one side. It can sound harsh to come out with 'what makes it fair?' or 'why do you believe it is fair?', so people who are excessively worried about hurting the relationship don't ask it – to their detriment.

112. **Fait accompli**:

As they say, 'better to apologise afterwards than ask permission before.' Some negotiators do this as their default style. They introduce changes to the contract and then you find out about them. They change the meeting room and you find out about it when you turn up at the agreed one and find no-one there. When something has been changed the new inertia of the situation means that it can be difficult to get it reversed. Doesn't always work but it works enough to be used with great regularity (at the cost of your relationship with the other side if you constantly use it.) Hence we stay with the same telephone provider despite the broken promises, cursing them and saying "I'll change provider next week." In the meantime they rack up the money.

113. **Fake smile:**

This refers to two different tricks, the mild one and the strong one. The mild one refers to the fact that even fake smiles (unless they are very, very obvious and/or condescending) have a tendency to provoke a smile from the other person (unless you are smiling like an idiot for the entire length of the negotiation). Provoking reciprocal smiles in the other person helps to create a more positive atmosphere in which to conduct the negotiation (it is hard to smile and be in a bad mood).

The strong trick is where you laugh at their jokes, smile with them encouragingly and pretend to be a friend with all the advantages that accrues in a negotiation. The reality is you are a snake waiting to bite. In the high powered and back stabbing business world in which many people operate this is standard practice.

114. **False deadlines:**

Real deadlines are so effective that people use false ones all the time. You probably already do. I know people who use them with their own families when travelling by telling them the flight is an hour before it actually is, just to get them to move and out the door. Test your counterpart's deadlines (not flight times!) in a negotiation if they don't suit you. Rarely are they fixed in stone. See **deadlines**.

115. **False logic:** see **Logic traps**

116. **False memories:**

Oh, how fickle is man! How many times have you dealt with someone who has a completely different memory of an event to you? In a negotiation this can ruin a deal completely and can be very frustrating unless of course you are the one who is 'mis-remembering' what was agreed earlier. If no notes are being taken you can remember what was said as much as you want and then retract concessions you have made on the basis that the other side isn't giving you what you wanted. This is not a good tactic to adopt continuously as you will build up a reputation for being untrustworthy and unreliable, but used selectively it can be an effective way of backtracking.

117. **False trail**: See **Red Herring**

118. **Fame**:

This has two branches, both related. The first application of the fame principle is to entice them by saying how they will be famous within their company for having reeled in the big fish' or the one 'that always gets away'. The other use of fame is to say that when other companies hear you are doing business with "*Mega Inc.*" then they will flock to you as well. Both branches of fame carry a cost (you sell at a lower price!)

119. **Fatigue**:

One of the enemies of all negotiators, especially those with more experience, but further on in years. Studies have shown that "when people are tired, they're likely to be in a heightened state of gullibility because of the diminished cognitive energy and motivation that exhaustion produces.' If you do not have breaks planned, a room where you can rest easily at night, and the negotiations are stressful and long you will find that your ability to negotiate/calculate/reason is reduced. If the other negotiation team can ensure that you do not get breaks, little sleep and are under constant pressure then you will be at a serious disadvantage. Recognise this and plan to create space for yourself.

120. **Fear**:

If you are frightened then you magnify negative consequences and threats and diminish your view of positive effects. Your thinking processes slow down. You are half the negotiator that you normally would be. Fear is wielded by unscrupulous competitive negotiators. It can come in the form of **threats** (veiled or direct) physical intimidation, references to everything that could go wrong if a deal isn't reached, **blackmail** etc. All of this is bad enough when it comes from the other side, but when it comes from you or your own team it can be even worse. Take steps to control your fear in a negotiation and avoid making your position even worse.

121. **Feel, felt, found formula:**

We understand how you feel, other clients felt the same when we showed them the proposal at first but then they found that it was the ideal solution for them. This successful formula shows empathy, shows that you have experience in this area and also shows that if the solution works for other people it will work for you, despite any natural misgivings you might have.

122. **Final offer:**

By stating this you are effectively saying that you won't make any more concessions and that you can't do any better. Well, that's the theory. I've witnessed negotiations where one side has said three times that an offer was their final one. If you do this then it is like crying wolf and you can never get the other side to believe you. A final offer should be your final offer. Having said that, there are entire cultures that seem to do this and you simply have to take the expression 'final offer' with a pinch of salt every time you hear it.

123. **Financial year:**

Understand what the financial year is for the people you are dealing with. That way you can avoid the **'empty pockets'** argument. When you know what the financial year is for them you can try and start negotiating at the end of it so that you can close the deal when the year has started and they have money in the bank again (and they will have budgeted for this at the *end* of the previous financial year)

124. **Flattery:**

It works. Sad but true. There are experts at this and they automatically make the other people feel good. We have a terrible tendency to shoot the messenger when the news is bad but when the news is good we see the other person in a different light. The good new doesn't even have to be sincere. If we make them feel good then they are more inclined to be generous with us in return

125. **Flexibility:**

This isn't a dirty trick - it's a simple common sense strategy to adopt in a negotiation. If you go in with a fixed position– and what you want doesn't match the other side's needs exactly, then you only have two choices, concede and lose face or walk out with no agreement. Going in with a flexible attitude means that you are ready to adjust, and prod and poke your proposal into a shape that fits the needs of both sides.

126. **Flinch and wince**:

Some people use this tactic so often in a negotiation that they end up looking constipated. Every time the other side makes a proposal you simply let an expression of pain cross your face or make a suitable sound (indrawn breath, hissing through your teeth, or 'ouch'). You are signalling to the other side that they shouldn't push harder, or maybe that they should even back off a little with their demands. Yet you haven't actually argued with anything they've said. This can stop **the Brooklyn optician** in his tracks, or signal a **major sacrifice** in the coming.

127. **Follow-up**:

Few negotiations are once off affairs. You don't end the relationship when you sign on the dotted line. It is always useful to look to the future (the next negotiation after this one) and plan accordingly. That involves sending a Thank You note, a small gift (even better if you have built up enough of a relationship to send it to the other side for their children) or some other way of showing your appreciation and friendship. This reaffirms the relationship and ensures that there is a greater chance that the deal will be implemented properly on their side.

128. **Foot in the door:**

Literally or metaphorically, they are both effective. When we say 'literally' we are not talking about the old door-to-door salesman trick (which was extremely effective when it was used) of jamming your foot in the door so the homeowner could not close it while you rattled off your spiel about whatever product you were trying to push on them.

Here we are talking about the advantage you having of being physically present. If you manage, get in the same room as the person you want to negotiate with, then you have a tremendous advantage over someone else with a similar product who is doing everything by mail and phone.

The other meaning of 'foot in the door' relates to the psychology of achieving small concessions first. Studies show that these small concessions on their part make it more likely that bigger concessions are later made when requested. Even when it is something as innocuous as asking them for a coffee and a pen to write with this can be effective.

129. **Force Majeure:**

Find out exactly what this means when you are signing a contract. You don't want to find out that everything can be attributed to an Act of God ("I didn't pay you on time and invested all your money in the Cayman Islands instead because God told me to do it!"). Also try and get your own Force Majeure expanded to include anything and everything.

130. **Force projection:**

Marching in front of the manager's window with placards reading 'We know where you live and we will burn your house down' would be an extreme example of force projection. . Lifting the phone in front of them and starting to dial the number of a boss/third party etc. can also be force projection. Calling a general meeting of all involved on your side, especially with television cameras rolling, can also be designed to make them take your threats more seriously. This can be taken as a form of **Coercive** power.

131. **Friendship**:

Friends can be as much trouble as enemies on occasion. They can call in debts, they can ask you to treat them better, to be 'kind' and go easy on them, to ask for favours. You may make all of these concessions if you feel the relationship is more important than the issues you are conceding. The problem truly arises when the friendship has been faked, when it is a one way street and that all you get from the other side is the appearance of friendship. There are negotiators who use this as their strategy. They wine and dine you, confide 'secrets' to you, have everything in common with you, laugh at all your jokes etc. In return you make concessions. When the time comes for them to give something more substantial in return there is always some excuse given and you are left with nothing. See **Fake Smile**.

132. **Full stomach:**

People argue less when they have a nice full stomach. A negotiation just after a heavy meal is generally less contentious.   People are a little sleepier, a little more content and sometimes that can be all the difference that you need.

133. **Funny money:**

Do you understand Net Present Value?   Discount Value? Hedges? Swaps? Compound interest rates?   Well, if you do and the other side doesn't, there is great room for offering what appears to be an attractive offer for them in the short term but that suit you in the long term. If you are not good at maths and don't understand financial instruments then be very careful of having the wool pulled over your eyes by people who do. Money is not always just money. A dollar today is not the same as a hedged yen with a buy back option tomorrow.

G

---

134. Get the ball rolling:

Negotiations can take on their own momentum and something that seemed impossible at the outset can be successfully resolved if the right atmosphere is created. Some negotiators are experts at making and getting small concessions at the beginning of the negotiation. This creates a feeling of 'Now, that wasn't so difficult, was it? Why don't we try something bigger?'

135. Get the other side to commit first:

There are those who prefer to set the price first (those who **anchor**) and those who prefer to set the price second (those who **Bracket**). By getting the other side to commit first you can stay flexible, you can bracket, and you get an idea of what they are thinking. This is especially useful if you don't have any idea what a normal price is and you want them to indicate how they are thinking. The idea is that if they go lower than you would expect you can haggle them up. If they go higher than you would have expected you win.

136. **Gifts**:

"Beware of Greeks bearing gifts." The origin of this phrase goes back to the Trojan War. We all know how that ended. First rule, if your counterparts leave a large wooden horse outside your company headquarters, don't bring it inside.

A free gift is rarely in fact free in a negotiation. It has been shown that NGO's and charities effectively raise money by sending you letters with a small gift inside. The reason they do this is because it has been demonstrated that there is a much greater chance that people will donate money as a result (far in excess of the value of the small gift, in fact). The other problem with gifts is that after you have accepted them you are told that it was never a gift in the first place. 'Hey, I gave you that X, don't you think it's about time you paid me back with Y?' See **Reciprocity** and **Big favour, little favour.**

137. **"Give it to me straight"**:

This is a very frank statement that invites an open and honest answer. However it doesn't mean that the person saying it will open up in return. People who use this very often get information from the other side and then give nothing back.

138. **Give me your best price:**

If you are a buyer this is fine (especially in a competitive, haggling negotiation), if you are a vendor this can be a nightmare question. It focuses the debate immediately on price as the key issue and almost makes it a prerequisite for continuing the negotiation. You can justify the price as many ways as you want but if they keep coming back at you with that price then) you may find yourself in a price war with lesser quality competitors and on the defensive, trying to justify your higher price. This line can cut through padding, your confidence and your schmoozing. It sounds like 'give it to me straight' but with a laser beam. As a vendor you should do everything to avoid being reduced to a commodity that simply trades on price (unless you are clearly the cheapest on the market and that is your Unique Selling Proposition) as not only does this reduce any margins you might build in but it also enables the side with most power (generally, but not always, the buyer) to simply go into a straight haggle weighted in their favour. A slight variation is 'Give me your best offer' when it is a negotiation that has little to do with money. See **'You'll have to do better than that'** and **'Differentiate or Die'**.

139. **"Go easy on me":**
Pity works *for* some and works *on* some. By mixing the relationship with the issues you can persuade the other side not to ask for more because they feel sorry for you. I know some people who say 'Go easy on me' regardless of the request that has been made. When used as a default line in every situation it could have the opposite effect and people end up refusing to make concessions *and* hating you.

140. **Golden Bridge:**

If you corner a rat it will fight. When making a proposal that is quite aggressive always allow some wiggle and escape room for the other side. Gently does it. Give them a golden bridge which they can use to escape. That means when they accept the deal they feel they are doing so voluntarily (even if that is an illusion), rather than having to take the choice. There is a greater chance that they will stick to the deal later if they feel they haven't been forced into accepting it. "Listen, let me give you some time to think about it. You don't have to accept this deal if you don't want to."   See **Back Off**.

141. **Golf:**

In many countries and many industries a lot of the negotiations happen in apparently 'non-business environments'.   Many business people take it for granted that in their own backyard it is normal to do business over lunch or on the golf course, and then they forget to investigate what would be the equivalent in the place where they are going.

This is important, as it may determine whether you bring someone on the team who can drink a lot of vodka, sing a lot of karaoke or knows a lot about rugby – or it will tell you what to be prepared for yourself. You should always remember that a negotiation never starts and stops at the door to the meeting room.

142. **Good cop bad cop:**

Wonderful tactic - a true classic. Good Cop, bad cop tactic is still used, to excellent effect in negotiations and interrogations around the world. You confide in the good cop, you even get the good cop to negotiate with the bad cop for you, you ask the good cop for advice on what you should do. You lose the negotiation.

143. **Guilt:**

This refers to two things; yours and theirs. Listen to your own, it will guide you well in the long run if not in the short run (you have to sleep with yourself for the rest of your life, whatever about anyone else). It is also a good indicator that something is not right with the deal. The other type of guilt is theirs, mentions of "how can you sleep at night" etc. might be enough to make them back off an aggressive or especially greedy stance when all the power is in their corner and none in yours.

H

---

144. Haggle with a hobgoblin:

If someone smelly, with black teeth and strange liquids leaking from their body and dressed in scraps and rags clings on to you then you would be forgiven by everyone if you paid them to release you. In a negotiation some people make you feel extremely uncomfortable in different ways without necessarily intimidating you. They may have terrible body odour, cough constantly in your direction without covering their mouth, never make eye contact with you, sit too close to you, etc. in short anything that makes your skin crawl and want to finish the negotiation as fast as possible instead of examining every line of the contract carefully or dragging discussions out. When the contract is signed the frog sometimes turns into a prince, the cough clears up, eye contact is made again and they become extremely charming. If that ever happens then try and rip up the contract before you leave the room!

145. Haggler's Universe

Reduce everything to one issue (normally price) and then start using every pressure or guilt tactic you know to get them to settle close to you, at the same time coming down a little for them so you have **made them work** but they feel they have wrangled something from you. This is especially useful if you have all the power, if you know the real price and they don't, if you are dealing with people who have no information (or possible access to it) about comparative prices or sources of supply and you are dealing with other people who may actually like to haggle). If the people you are dealing with like to haggle then you will not hurt the relationship. If the people you are dealing with do not like to haggle then they will settle very close to your **Anchor** simply to stop the process. Surprisingly easy skills to develop if you don't have them already. The first rule is to treat the negotiation like a game and enjoy the process of haggling itself as pure theatre.

146. **Halo effect:**

This refers to the fact that one salient feature, (generally) positive, of another person stands out and colours our image of all their other attributes. The most cited example is the fact that very good looking people are generally considered more intelligent and trustworthy than less attractive people. If you are lucky enough to have a feature like that, be sure to leverage it. However be wary of being blinded by their halo. It helps to write down on a piece of paper all the attributes of the other side (physical, personality, qualifications, experience etc. and then eliminate their strongest card. Then look at everything they have left and see how they add up in isolation. This can help you from falling into the **Honey Trap** or being fooled by an **Expert**.)

147. **Hands tied:**

You can't budge, make concessions or help the other side because 'your hands are tied'. This means you have no money, no authority, strict orders from above, whatever you need to give the excuse that you are not in a position to change. The expression 'I'm afraid my hands are tied' allows you to stick to your guns without damaging the relationship.

148. **Hedging:**

Insurance, lifeboat clauses, penalty clauses, conflict resolution clauses, force majeure clearly indicated etc. Design the deal to protect yourself if anything goes wrong. Never assume that the negotiation has finished when you have signed the contract. Instead of crying afterwards when they do a **9/10s** on you then hedge early.

149. **"Help me out this time and I'll see you right next time":**

Unless you are very good friends and you have a relationship of complete trust then be very careful of this one. There is rarely a next time. Either you never get to negotiate with this person again or they have a raft of excuses to explain why they can't help you when next time comes around. Whatever concessions you have made in this negotiation will lose value in their eyes the moment it comes to returning the favour.

Exceptions: in some situations it may be normal to build up mutually beneficial relationships where people take alternating hits for each other (think friends who are prepared to make sacrifices for each other over the years). With someone who you can see is a person of their word (good luck recognising that!) then you know they will 'see you right the next time' and may even do you one better due to the trust you have placed in them. As a general rule, though, watch out!

150. **Help me to help you:**

This is the most basic principle of many negotiations and yet people often forget how essential it is to any agreement where both parties voluntary accept the deal. If they make money, you make money. If they are happy with the agreement and do not invade your territory again, then you are happy. By using this phrase you are trying to get them to open up to you about their interests from self-interest.

A competitive negotiator is only using this line to prise open the oyster but an Eagle negotiator is genuinely interested in a win-win deal for everyone and says this to point out that uncovering interests is the best way to find a solution for everyone.

151. **"Help me to understand":**

This is when you pretend to be a principled negotiator. They say that they are interested in knowing what the motivating factors behind your position are or that they genuinely want to help you out but they need to know what is going on in your heads or in your organisation. When they have found out they twist the screws and all empathy/sympathy/kindness is gone.

152. **High ball:**

Come in with an excessively high figure. If they accept it, great, you are much richer than you expected. If they don't accept it but agree to negotiate then you have anchored (see **Anchoring**) the figure much higher than you would have. Coming in with a high ball may also shock them out of any comfortable expectations they had when they came into the negotiation. However, if you have no power, they have an excellent **BATNA**, your counterpart knows the true price/value of whatever you are selling/buying, or you are in a culture where entering with a ridiculously high figure is not acceptable then don't risk it.

153. **Higher authority:**

Having plenipotentiary powers (being able to sign off on any deal with the full powers of your organisation) can be extremely dangerous. Under pressure, influenced by short term pleasures, or simply conned, you can take decisions in the moment that you will regret at your leisure. Having a Higher Authority (a boss, a board of directors, a spouse) that you have to check with before taking a decision can help you protect yourself from ill-advised decisions. That higher authority might even be invented and when you go outside to call your boss it might just be the talking clock you call but at least you are no longer under direct pressure to take a decision and you have the perfect excuse to say "sorry, I can't give you that 15% discount you're looking for". Try to avoid calling your boss, fictitious or not, in front of a very pushy negotiator or they might insist that you pass them your phone. Whether they speak to your boss or simply hear 'it is now 12.30 in Australia' it does not bode well for you.

154. **Hire an expert**: See **Third Party Expert**

155. **Honey trap**:

Seduction works. If you are seduced by the other side (whether sex is involved or not) then you will make concessions that you would not make otherwise. This can happen to both sexes. It can be very sad to witness someone falling into the Honey Trap. It would be even sadder if it's you in the trap.

156. **Hospitality**:

And every glass of wine you gargle and every sugary doughnut you munch at the free buffet can and will be used against you in a court of law! Yes, it's great at the time but after all is said and done, the food and drink you consumed and every helicopter ride you take to every private island, adds up to a tiny percentage of the discount you will be expected to give in return. See **reciprocity** and **gifts**.

157. **Hostage negotiating**:

They cut off the light and the electricity and then make you give up a hostage for every blanket, gallon of water and pizza they give you (having profiled the hostage takers as rational and not mentally disturbed – otherwise it's a different type of negotiation). In a negotiation this means that you make them pay for absolutely every concession you give them, no matter how small.

158. **Hot potato:**

They have a problem and they make it yours. "I'm afraid my boss said that I was crazy to accept that offer so I won't be able to fulfil the terms of the contract after all." "I'm afraid our biggest supplier hasn't paid us yet so we won't be able to pay you this month." "Our warehouse manager broke the model you gave us so you are going to have to give us another one to replace it." The answer to all hot potatoes should be "How is this my problem? !" Unless of course you have no choice but to accept it because you will never get your money any other way or it is worth your while to keep this client sweet. In that case argue how they give you the hot potato: For example: "That's fine but we are going to have to add on an extra 5% to cover our own overdraft expenses to pay our own suppliers."

159. **"How could you say no?":**

This is said in complete disbelief. The hint that you think they are mad is laced through your words. The aim is to make them believe that you have just made them the best offer in the history of man and they are just too blind to see it. If they come back with rational and logical reasons then you have garnered useful information which is much more valuable to you than a simple 'no' (though not as valuable as them recanting and accepting your magical offer)

160. **Humour:**

If you have a good sense of humour you'll know how a joke or funny comment or even a raised eyebrow at the right time can break a situation of tension, get the other side on board and turn conflict into a positive problem solving atmosphere. Try to make yourself funnier if you want to, read books of humorous quotations and joke books. And then make sure that you are in a culture that will accept you telling a joke about an Australian, an Englishman and an American walking into a bar.

161. **Hunger:**

Negotiate through lunchtime without a break. Don't drink water for a prolonged period. Don't have a cigarette break if you are a nicotine addict. Now try and concentrate. Not as easy before is it? Would anyone be so cruel as to eat before they met you and then happily not let you take a break?   Have a negotiation in a place where you can't smoke and keep on going and going? Surely not. But just in case, just in case, bring a sandwich in your bag and some nicotine chewing gum in your pocket.

162. **Hurt and betrayed:**

If they have said something (doesn't matter if they have promised it or not) and then can't give it you can act hurt and betrayed. This is good to use in response to "**I'm afraid my boss won't let me**" and especially useful if you can combine with **guilt** and **crocodile tears.**

163. **Hustle close:**

This is fine for something small and a one off negotiation. Don't give them time to think and then rush them through at the end, getting them to sign in a hurry before the deal ends and someone else comes in to buy It can backfire though if the person does not like to be rushed or if you are going to be part of an on-going relationship with them.

I

---

164. "I'd love to but":

"I'd love to buy your product, I think it's great, I can really see how it would work in our company, in fact I'd love to buy thirty, it's just that....our budget has been signed off for the year and we don't have enough at its current price OR my manager told me that we can't pay anything over X OR your competitor was in last week and he offered us the same product/service for half the price OR we'd need it by tomorrow and can't pay any more than the price we agreed."

The other party hooked and excited and just might come down to whatever you're asking for. If not you can always backtrack with **"Let me see what I can do".**

165. I feel your pain:

....followed by *but*. You are showing empathy, showing understanding, *but* you're not going to budge an inch. Don't take it hard, it's not personal, it's just business.

166. "I'm afraid my boss won't agree":

This is exactly the same as 'I'm afraid my mom won't let me'. If it was up to you, no problem, but your 'higher authority' vetoes whatever you agreed to and it doesn't damage your relationship, because it's not your fault that you can't follow up on what you agreed to do. Cue thirty years later. "Of course we can give you this, that and the other in return, Mr. Client. Satisfied. Great. So you're happy to sign. Ok. Let me just go and check the papers." Ten minutes pass. Mr. Client has had plenty of time to visualise him/herself living in house/driving car/using blender, in his/her favourite colour and at a fantastic price. They have already brought it home in their own heads. Then you come back and say 'I'm afraid the boss said I can't give you the 10% discount. It will have to be 8% I'm afraid, but it's still a great deal. Is that okay?"

167. I never loved you:

You negotiate with one company simply to get information to help you with another negotiation, the real one. You find out what a good price could be, or what other features are on offer, or to show the other company that you are serious about going elsewhere. If you are the person on the receiving end you are sure that everything is going fine until *bam*, they leave you without even giving you the courtesy of a Dear John letter.

168. I really wouldn't feel right about doing this:

When someone says "no" due to their conscience. Of course you can't argue with someone's conscience ("No, do it, feel guilty and unethical, do it for me"). The problem is that the person's conscience could be telling them not to accept a lower price as they would be hurting their shareholders/manager/mother. If you can think of no good reason to defend your arguments for why you shouldn't accept an offer then go with this one.

169. I understand and....:

When you are contradicting someone instead of saying I understand *but* I think you'll find ABC" it is better to say "I understand *and* I think you'll find ABC." Why? Because people hear the But in the first sentence and get revved up for your argument and for their counterargument. With the second sentence they listen to what you are saying, think that you are agreeing with them and very often they see the sense in your argument.

170. "I understand how you feel. "X person" felt the same way, but they found....": see **feel, felt, found** formula.

171. I'll think about it and get back to you later:

Later could mean never or it could simply give me the time to think without being pressured. When you use the tactic one way it can create problems for you because you are essentially saying "No" but your counterpart doesn't hear that and may continue to hassle you. The other way gives you time to think, without being under pressure.

172. "I'm sorry, I've made a mistake":

This could be genuine, and certainly worth trying if it has happened to you (they may not accept your apology and prefer to keep whatever you gave them by mistake. Only the context and whether you have a contract will let you know if that's going to happen). Very often it can be used in conjunction with **deliberate mistake** and **I'm afraid my boss won't let me.**

173. **If and then:** see **conditional concessions**

174. **If I could show you..., would you...?:**

Typically used in sales this is a way of finding out if they are prepared to take a buying decision or not. "If I can show you that this car is the car for you, would you be prepared to buy it today?", "If I could show you that we are better, cheaper and quicker than all our competitors, would you be in a position to sign today?" See **Commitment traps** for other uses of this. If they say 'yes' then you have them. If they say 'no' then you can ask them what it would take. You gain valuable information regardless of the answer (try a **hustle close**, for example)

175. **"If I remember correctly":**
This phrase would precede a line like 'you mentioned ten and not fifteen trucks.' It may be useful for stating your position without creating conflict.

176. **"If it was me....":**
As in, "I'm not telling you what to do but you would be mad not to do the following...." Again this is a way of advising the other side without actually telling them. The idea behind this is to avoid imperatives and should-ing (you should do this, you should do that), both of which can get hackles up in many cultures. Again you will probably end with "of course, it's your choice." Do not repeat this sentence very often because you are simply inviting the response 'But you're not me, are you? No you're not. So I'm going to do the exact opposite of whatever you are 'suggesting'."

177. **"If you were in my shoes":**
This is specifically asking the person to be sympathetic to your needs. You follow this statement with "then you would see that I have no choice here", or "I can't go any lower" etc. etc. You can work this with **"go easy on me",** **guilt** or **"my boss is a bastard."**

178. "I have two kids too":

"Hey, I'm just like you, I have two kids too. And because I'm just like you, you know you can trust me. And whatever I do, or believe about a product or service, will be a good guide for how you should think. Why? Because you have two kids too. Unfortunately, when they are saying they 'have two kids too' they're not always telling the truth.

However if you do have something in common with the other side it doesn't hurt to mention it (unless you are talking about cars and you suddenly interject 'hey, remember you said you liked knitting, well so do I"). In fact the reason it is abused is because it is so effective. When used honestly it can create rapport and understanding. Studies have shown that we are more influenced by people who are like us. See **in-group-out-group.**

179. "I'm not going to tell you...":

We all know what's coming next, don't we? I'm not going to tell you what it is but it probably involves me saying something or telling you to something anyway, which you will be psychologically influenced by but which I have definitely not told you to do!

You tell people you are not going to tell them exactly what you then go on to tell them. This is often combined with an **embedded command**. Some people exist in a world where they manipulate absolutely everyone around them with this formula and then deny that they have ever instructed a single person in their lives.

180. **I'm only a simple foreigner:**

Similar to **Lost In Translation** but much more general. Also combines **playing dumb** without such a loss of face. You can make mistakes and put it down to culture (when it is not). You can ask them to explain in detail every point because it's different to the way you do things at home (even if it's not). That way you can see how much they know and happily keep your professional credibility, and you can ask as many questions as you want.

181. **Increase the issues:**

See **adding and subtracting.** It is easier to create packages if you have several issues to discuss (and hence easier to **Waterbed** it). A common piece of advice is to try to avoid issues being reduced to one single issue (for example, price) with two opposing positions and then "1,2,3 – let's haggle like camel traders. You start by offering 20 and I'll come back with 5". Increasing the number of issues helps to avoid this happening because you can decrease your offer in some areas while increasing it in others until you have a deal that suits you both.

182. **Increase the size of the pie:**

Increasing the size of the pie is a key objective of the principled school of negotiations (it isn't always possible but it makes sense to always *look*). Haggling normally presupposes a fixed pie – what I get you lose. Increasing the pie takes the opposite view. The famous example of the orange illustrates this.

Two people are negotiating over an orange. A fair solution might be to let one person cut the orange and the other person chooses which half they want. However increasing the pie might involve both parties discussing their interests. One states that they want the orange peel to make a cake, while the other says that they want the orange to eat. They both get "all" of the orange in this case. The size of the pie (or orange) has been increased as a result of the negotiation.

Use creativity to try and find value for the other side in things that have little or no importance for you. Or ways of creating value for both sides from the same deal.

183. **Information**:

The more information you have (as a general rule) the better. Spend as much time as you need gathering it. Keep eyes and ears open before during and after. This does mean checking out information on the internet that relates to them. It does not necessarily mean spying on them with a professional agency.

184. **In-group-out-group:**

Belonging to the same group creates union and concessions. Studies have shown that the moment people identify you as part of their group they are more prepared to reward you (and conversely if they have identified you as definitely not part of their group they are readier to punish you). Find things in common and focus on bonds that bring you together in the same group. Even using 'we' language can help create this feeling. Extreme versions and difficult to fake, would be clubs (from local football clubs to country clubs). See **'I have two kids too**.'

185. **Interpreter**:

This does not mean having an actual interpreter (see **Two Translators**). This tactic is where there is someone on your team specifically because they speak the other side's language so they can listen in when the other team is discussing issues. Give that person another job title (floor manager, junior sales agent etc.) and make no offer to help the other side with translations at any point because it is better if the other side never find out that someone on your team understood what they were discussing in their own language at the table.

186. **"Is that your best offer?"   "Is that the best you can do?"**:

If they say yes then they run the risk of deadlock. If they say no then they will give you a better offer. It is amazing how many times the answer to these questions is "Let me see what I can do for you." If they only knock a tiny percentage off or add a small extra you have gained something for nothing.

187. **"Is there anything that would stop you agreeing to…"**:
Find out, if possible, anything that would stop them taking a decision that day. Your objective here could be to find out what their needs are, or what their ratification process is. If you find out what their possible problems are then you can design your proposal to assuage their fears. If you discover that their ratification process is quite complex then you will have to make sure that you do not go down to your bottom line in the very first round of negotiations because there will be more to come. If they say that they have no problems taking a decision and then go back on their word at the end of your discussions you have also gained valuable information (in which case your offer is a time dependent one which will not last indefinitely into the future). See **'If I could show you, would you?'**

188. **It's a deal, let's negotiate:**
This tactic is sometimes cultural rather than competitive. It is the tendency to negotiate a deal, sign the contract, go home and then start to negotiate the implementation of what was agreed formally. If you are all in the same country and you have a water tight contract then it can be easy to combat this tactic (i.e. go to court) However if you are dealing with people in another country you might find it difficult to tackle this if they start **nibbling** (especially if they are using this tactic with **9/10s**). Always design an agreement thinking about how you can implement it, do not rely on the contract being enough.

189. **It's ok not to.....:**

By telling people that they have a choice, that they don't have to do something, you're making it easier for them to say yes. As simple as that. "It's ok not to believe me, I'd like you to use this and tell me if it works or not." This takes pressure off sensitive or trigger happy opponents.

190. **"It's that easy!":**

Also see **Simple Solutions**. If you make it easy for the other side then you can get things that you normally wouldn't. You go to their office, you bring all the information that is needed (all thoroughly researched and presented in a reader friendly format), you make sure that you will deliver everything and bear the costs of freight and insurance, you assure them that they will have absolutely no problems – just leave it all up to you. And then remember to charge them the sun, moon and stars for their laziness.

J

191. **Just a little servant**:

Instead of pretending you have authority when you have none (**Paper Crown**) you say that you have no authority when you do (little servant). That way you are not forced into taking a decision due to the pressure of the moment and you can buy time when you go to consult with a fictitious **Higher Authority**.   Of course you will then have to accept that you run the risk that they will want to bypass you and speak directly to that decision maker. Have your excuses ready! Also, take into account possible damages to your credibility and status sensitive cultures.

192. **Just because it's you:**

When you feel you have to make a unilateral reduction from a **padded price** to secure a deal make sure that they know they are getting a special deal because of your good relationship with them. If you want to build up goodwill for future negotiations, if you are doing a **concession close** or if you are doing a **Last concession lost** with them then this is fine but as a general rule all concessions should be conditional (and avoid at all costs trying to turn **Tigers into Vegetarians.)**

193. **Just say No:**

Practice saying this. If you are a person that rarely says No then when you do say NO it sounds stronger, more forceful and more final. But you have to be able to say it. You should practice this in conjunction with **'I wouldn't feel comfortable doing that.'**

K

---

194. **Keeping you waiting:**

You are left in the waiting room while they finish whatever meeting they are in (or you are simply told "Mrs. Hertzenweger will be with you in a moment" without explanation.) It drags on beyond what is generally acceptable in your culture (this length of time changes from country to country). Finally they come out and greet you without a single explanation or apology. They have just psychologically shown that you are inferior to them. In retaliation, I have seen some people be on the phone whenever the person they are visiting comes out to greet them and they turn the tables by lifting a finger and mouthing 'just a minute'. My own personal suggestion is to simply bring other documents with you that you have to work on, try meditation or read a book and feel like a million dollars whenever they have stopped playing their waiting game. For these kinds of tricks you can choose to be influenced or not, this isn't real power, this is just sleight of hand power (though it can add up if you are not careful)

195. **Kissing babies:**

Creating bonds with your negotiator through the people around them, gifts for their spouse and/or children, asking after their parents etc. In some cultures doing a favour like offering to add a ramp (free of charge) for the other negotiator's grandfather's wheelchair so they can get in and out of the office block you are building for them might be the tiny goodwill gesture that gets them on side. Then **reciprocity** and **friendship** kicks in. (We are not advocating going as far as **Bribery** here)

196. **Know where you're going**:

Basics of negotiation preparation. Have an idea of what success looks like for you and what your underlying interests are, and know when you have reached them (and when you have not). This avoids you haggling like a demon and then discovering that you may have won the 'haggle' but not achieved your goal. It also means that there is less of a chance of you suffering from **Winners' curse** if you got what you wanted, but very easily.

L

197. Labelling:

People's perception is often influenced simply by the label you put on something, rather than the thing itself. You might be sceptical until you think of the money spent on packaging, or the money paid to consulting companies for choosing the right name for a new company.

Studies have shown that by calling someone generous at the beginning of a negotiation encourages them to act accordingly. Try the same with flexible, open minded, patient etc.

Research has also been carried out with negotiation role plays that demonstrate when the negotiation was labelled as something like 'The Wall Street game' people were more competitive than when it was called the 'Community game'. When negotiating you would be better calling the negotiation 'a problem solving session' or simply a 'meeting' rather than a negotiation, which generally conjures up opposing forces and may put your counterpart on guard before you even started asking for concessions.

198. **Last concession lost:**

Even if you have won everything you wanted, wrung every concession possible out of them and given three turnips and a small rock in exchange for an office block it is very often the last concession made that is remembered. If you are going to make any unilateral, goodwill gestures try to make them now (). After all that is said and done, this will be impression they are left with when they walk away, and you always want them to feel as if they have won – regardless of the reality of the deal..

199. **Last minute changes**:

Everything is agreed, everyone is happy and then a few modifications have to be made before the contract is signed, as circumstances have changed. After fighting like there's no tomorrow in the exchange stage you then accept these changes like a meek little kitten, so you can sign the bleeding contract once and for all. See **Quivering Quill.**

200. **Launching a tangent:**

You start talking about a subject that is only remotely related to the subject to avoid discussing the issue at hand. You can do this for several reasons, to avoid the conflict of a direct 'no' and also to set up a potential decoy or straw man that you can give in on later, in return for something else.

201. **Lawyer:**

In many countries it is not only a good idea to "lawyer up", it is in fact essential (from a legal and a common sense point of view). However even in countries/situations where it is not a strict requirement it can still be a good idea to bring a lawyer. Sometimes the very fact that you have said you are going to get your lawyer to glance over some documents will mean that the other side will not put in 'suspect clauses'. Getting a lawyer to draw up documents also permits you to cloak a contract in legalese and make it difficult for the other side to understand, and argue with. Be careful of bringing lawyers into the equation at the wrong time though as they may break an incipient rapport you are trying to build with your counterpart.

202. **Leaking:**

Why would you leak information? So that the other side's stakeholder's demand for the deal to be broken?; To get your own side so angry that you go back to the negotiating table with your hands tied?; For money?; To destroy other factions on your team?

The tactic is common and simple, the motivation could be quite complex. To make leaks less likely (especially accidental ones) you should have a strict policy on talking to the media/outside people (difficult to enforce), you may even need all the people involved to sign a confidentiality clause.

203. **Least effort:**

See **It's that easy!** Never underestimate people's desire to take short cuts) in today's hyper fast world where people often have more money than time. Laziness and speed, as we have seen, both carry a price. Offering a service that saves them mental and physical energy charges a dividend. Do this with people who have deep pockets and no time. It might even be your unique selling point.

204. **Legalise Cocaine!:**

Put a very contentious issue on the agenda. All the debate focuses on this. You finally give it up. When they then try to take another much less contentious issue off the agenda you then argue that you have already made a concession with the 'cocaine' issue. Ironically enough, I have been witness to people who were too successful in their defence of the 'cocaine' issue and ended up wondering how to get rid of it in the negotiation. If this happens to you, the solution is easy, you can always use it as a **straw man** later in the negotiation.

205. **Legitimate power:**

The cleanest type of power to have. You have legitimate power due to the authority granted to you by an official body (and authority that is directly relevant to this negotiation). Or perhaps you have been granted the right to take the final decision, to sign the contract, to tell people what to do, to reward or to punish. And because it is legitimate it is difficult to argue with (legitimate doesn't mean fair).

206. "Let me check my notes...:"

See **Magic Writing** plus **If I remember correctly**. If you have written it down (even if you had it wrong) you can make the other side look bad if you correct them on the basis of your notes, especially if you unscrupulously make it look like you are making a concession to them by giving into their 'lie' and agreeing to change your notes.

207.   "Let me see what I can do":

Major sacrifice, backtracking, regaining credibility, avoiding the **winner's frown**.

208. **Let me tell you a story**:

We are hardwired to understand stories, to be persuaded by stories, to remember stories. If you can give captivating stories of success cases, of people who didn't buy your product and were subsequently killed in a freak Hot Air Balloon disaster in Shanghai ("It happened to a friend of a friend") then you will find it much easier to persuade the mere mortals in front of you about the benefits of your proposal.

209. **Let them own the solution**:

Forget pride when you enter the negotiation. It shouldn't matter who gets the credit for the deal being a success, as long as you get what you want and what your organisation wants. If you let them feel they have come up with the winning proposal/solution all the better. They won't try and wriggle out of it later if they feel it was their idea. If they also feel that they have 'won' then all the better for you. They won't try and gouge more concessions out of you the next time.

210. **Let them save face**:

Avoid humiliation where possible (unless this is part of some elaborate strategy you have, perhaps **Good Cop/Bad cop**?) as you get very little, if anything, in return, and the other side will want to get revenge as quickly as possible. People can forgive most things in a negotiation but for most of us, humiliation isn't one of them. Even better than not humiliating them, let them save face. This could be the **Last Concession Lost**, or not enforcing a contract when there were clearly mistakes in it that would create terrible problems for the negotiator within their own organisation. If you are dealing with a normal person (who hasn't made a **deliberate mistake**) then the whole factor of **reciprocity** will kick in. There is a greater chance that trust will be built for future negotiations, that they will return the favour or at the very least they will do their best to implement the deal internally after the contract has been signed.

211. **Lifeboat clause:**

When you are writing up the contract make sure that you have a clause that ensures you are protected if they do not deliver on what they have promised (for example: if not paid within ten days then the price increases by 10% and no further products are sent, if not paid by 20 days then X mediator called in, if not paid by 40 days court case). If the issue of trust is brought up you can put it down to standard company policy, and besides they won't have to worry as, of course, they are extremely reliable ("aren't you?")

212. **Light in your eyes:**

You can do this the right way and the wrong way. The wrong way: They can walk into a room and be blinded immediately by light streaming in through the window and be completely disoriented. They then sit down, hackles raised, and start negotiating and when the tense bargaining stage of the negotiation has come around the sun has moved on and it is now blazing into your eyes.

Or else you can do it the right way – have the sun out of their eyes at the beginning when they enter wary and sniffing for a trap and then wait as the sun moves around and into their eyes when they have forgotten about it and are now trying to calculate under pressure.

213. **Link to their desires:**

Appeal to their emotions, base instincts and desires, and not just their logical, rational side. We are not robots and we take decisions based on the churning emotions created by a racing heart, hormones, adrenaline, bile and gastric acid. First the Heart and then the Head.

214. **Linking**:

Linking can be the idea of creating a package and building it up so that you are not beaten issue by issue. It can also be linking back to positive advances in the negotiation to show how far you have come, to encourage all parties to continue at the table.

215. **Listening**:

Listening, really listening, is not a dirty trick, it's common sense. The person who is able to listen better (and it is a skill you can learn) is at an automatic advantage in a negotiation. Stop thinking about what you are going to say next and how to defeat their arguments. Just listen and learn.

216. **Listening devices**:

Electronic spying. It is easy to hack into a cell phone for the right people so there are many high level meetings/military/police forces that insist on you leaving your mobiles outside when you go into the room where the negotiation is going to take place. Even with the phone turned off, unless the battery is taken out you can use the phone to listen to the people in the room. Then there's the speakerphone which is left on in the room where you are discussing sensitive aspects of the negotiation with your team. Or your phone is bugged, or your hotel room. Do you have a secure line or a way of ensuring that the room where you are having a caucus is clear of bugs? This may seem exaggerated paranoia to everyone except those who do it and those who have suffered it.

217. **Little by little:**

A combination of taking your time and simply trying to negotiate (patience!) every little item, one by one. This way you make sure that do everything right. If it is part of your strategy then it may also frustrate the other side (Tortoise style). It also warns them to not slip in any little surprizes as you will notice them, even in the small print.

A further aspect of little by little is gradually escalating commitments so they end up saying Yes to something big because they never said No to a thousand small things along the way. See **Brooklyn Optician** for a clearer example of this.

218. **Living with uncertainty:**

Some people can handle it, others can't, (see **Brinkmanship**.) Leaving things to the last minute, painting a **Rosy future** without worrying about the details is fine for some people but others are prepared to pay extra for security and certainty - now! That also means that in a negotiation where you can have the power to give certainty you can negotiate this point and get concessions in return for security.

"How much would you be willing to pay if I could guarantee you X, right here, right now?"

219. **Location**:

Playing at home gives tremendous room for tricks. You can ensure that the room is set up in a way that makes the visitors feel comfortable/uncomfortable. You can make the trip from their hotels to the meeting room a trip through paradise or a trek through hell. You can bring them to best restaurants or leave them munching on sandwiches in the corridor. You can keep them drinking until two in the morning with people they won't be negotiating with the next morning. . There is tremendous power here as context can make or break a negotiation. Don't make the mistake of dismissing location as unimportant.

220. **Logic traps:**

"If you are a carpenter then you will love this brand of cigarettes". "If you are a woman then you will love this brand of pick-up trucks." "If you have a penguin farm ...oh, you do?... then this fridge is for you.' By creating false logics you can trap the unwary. See **commitment traps**.

221. **Log rolling:**

You bundle a package and then happily throw away (well, let's be serious, you never *just* throw away concessions in a negotiation, see **conditional concession**) the ones of less importance to get movement going and get what you want on the issues of real importance to you.

222. **Look for no:**

Pushing for No very often gives you valuable information if you can get them to explain the thinking behind their No. Very often when people nod, or even say 'yes' it is not because they have any real intention of going with your proposal. They may be doing so out of a cultural or a personal bias against saying 'no'. They may simply mean that they understand, but are not necessarily interested. They may just be trying to humour you because they do not care enough to bother saying No.

Uncovering what their possible opposition or blocks to the deal are, means that you can push for genuine buy in, or abandon the deal at an earlier date, rather than trying to follow up after this meeting with several more, or discovering their objections when it comes to actually implementing the deal.

223. **Lost in translation:**

Many people believe that negotiating in another language only has disadvantages. There are ways to turn it to your advantage. You can pretend that you only understand what it suits you to understand, to apologise for mistakes made 'because you didn't understand', get them to repeat different points in different ways to help you catch the meaning (and also see if they give away more information). You can ignore certain points. You can get them to explain difficult words related to minor points in the negotiation ad nauseam ('I'm sorry, I still don't understand') in the hope that they might actually give up on whatever they are requesting.

224. **Low ball:**

Coming in with an excessively low price/offer in order to get them to reassess their expectations, throw them off, anchor them at a lower price, shock them. This is only effective if there aren't transparent prices that give the lie to your low ball.

M

---

225. Magic writing:

If I say something to you, you may believe me, or you may not, you may think I am a liar or I simply don't know what I am saying. However if I type up what I could have told you, put it on headed paper and possibly stamp it, or at the very least sign it, it takes on a greater power than the spoken word. Try to bring documents typed up (written is a poor second cousin in the 21st century) where ever possible (this goes double for the agenda). If they only have the 'spoken word' it doesn't have the same weight as whatever you have down on paper.

226. Major Sacrifice:

Some people go too far with this and make a huge drama over absolutely every single tiny miniscule concession they make. However as a rule in negotiations don't give things up happily with a shrug of your shoulders). Make the other side feel like they have twisted your arm and beaten you into submission. Let them feel that they have 'won' the negotiation. (See **Flinch and wince**) In bazaars around the world you are told how their entire families will sleep hungry that night because of the price they have given you. In offices from Trinidad to Tobago you are told that their boss is going to fire them for the deal you have carved (yes, carved) out of them.

227. **Make them work:**

Connected to major sacrifice is the idea of making them work to get the deal. It has been shown that people are happier if they have haggled you down (or up) from your original starting point. So much so that if you immediately offered them something better in Negotiation A they would not be as happy as they would be with a worse result and a struggle in Negotiation B. (This is partially to avoid the much cited **winners frown**).

228. **Massaging a big ego:**

An application of **flattery**. You build them up about their decision making power and their expertise. This then traps them when the time comes to take a decision (if they have a big ego they cannot admit that they need to ask someone else first, nor can they say they do not understand the terms as they have allowed themselves to be built up as the 'expert'.)

229. **Minimum Order:**

You will give them the price they are looking for, but on the condition that they have to order a certain, minimum amount. This is a reason all on its own, for **padding** a price in the first place. Of course giving a better price for a minimum amount is a discount just like 'pay in cash' or 'timely payment discount'.

230. **Mirroring and Pacing:**

Most commonly used by salespeople. They mirror your body language, language and intonation so that rapport is created between you. Then they change in the direction that suits their purposes – they speed up to get you more excited, change negative adjectives to positive, or simply uncross legs and arms and lean forward to get you do the same – and be physically more receptive to the deal.

231. **Missing person manoeuvre:**

You specifically leave out a key person in your team. This could be (most usually) the key decision maker. As a result it doesn't matter what is agreed there is no one at the table to ratify it (see **Higher Authority**). It could also be leaving out a specialist (finance director or lawyer) which means that the contract/papers will have to be taken away and studied (without pressure and in a quiet place) before the negotiation can go any further. It might even be the Bad Cop of the **Good cop, Bad cop** routine that you decide to leave at home (temporarily). They are a looming threat and through their distance, can make the negotiators present appear closer together.

232. **Money in the bank:**

If you have liquidity, if you can pay by cash and immediately or let them pay late because you have a cushion, this gives you greater leverage in the negotiation. See **COTS**.

233. **Musical Chairs:**

This involves changing negotiators. This isn't **tag team**ing per se. This could be for a variety of reasons: To avoid you getting too friendly with any single negotiator and using friendship against them; to confuse you because you never know what tactics to adopt; to use specialists in the different phases of the negotiation; to make it easier for them to play hardball with you as they don't know you well enough to feel any sympathy; and of course all the reasons of **Tag Team**.

234. **Mutual solutions:**

The best way, in any negotiation, to get what you want is to make sure they also get what you want. A key pillar of the Principled School of Negotiations (see the introduction of this book).

235. **My boss is a b*st*rd:**

What would possess someone from saying such a terrible thing? (Setting aside sharing the truth in a negotiation setting for a moment). In order to try and create a common bond with the other person (along the lines of 'I have two children, too') and to elicit sympathy and a lower price, perhaps? This is a very subtle version of **Good Cop, Bad Cop**, with the Bad cop never even coming to the police station that day.

236. **My daddy...:**

In a negotiation powerful family connections are called in regularly and you sometimes wonder who you are negotiating with, the negotiator in front of you or their parents' friends.

237. **"My friend Vincent...":**

Sometimes the allies of the negotiator you are dealing with are not the kind of people you want knowing about you. You might be dealing with an officially legitimate person. Their friend Vincent is less legitimate. At present you don't want Vincent to know where you live. The person you are dealing with has Vincent on speed dial 1. The very fact that they remark that 'Vincent would be very interested to hear what you have to offer' might be enough for you to drop your prices. You have three choices: drop your prices, do not do business with this person or make sure you have a friend who is also called Vincent.

238. **My hearing isn't very good:**

Similar to **playing dumb** but more along the lines of "I remember when we used to call MP3 players gramophones." You have to go easy on them because they are old. You have to speak louder and clearer. You have to explain everything in detail. You have to be sympathetic and give an old fellow a break. You should not at any point remember that this person was selling ice to the Inuit when you were in diapers, and perhaps even when your dad was in diapers. Nor should you point out that this negotiator probably sold your granny said diapers at a steep mark-up – "back when people used to stand behind a square cut out of cardboard and pretend they had a television".

Don't trust old negotiators! They were just as smart as you are when they were your age. And negotiators are like expensive wine, they get better with age.

N

---

239. **Never Say No:**

This can be a very frustrating strategy to come up against. They never actually agree, or sign the contract but they don't disagree with anything you say or directly say "no". Because they don't give you any objections you can't find out what their real interests are and therefore you never really close the deal. The exact opposite to **Always say No** with a different goal (not getting an agreement or giving away information as opposed to improving the offer)

240. **Never say Yes to the first offer:**

You might have to accept what they first offered you by the end of the negotiation, or even five minutes after it has started but don't automatically say 'yes' to whatever they say or they will fall prey to the **winner's frown**. If you start with an automatic Yes they may even start making their offer worse. Example:

'500'.

Fine

'Plus VAT'.

Ok.

'You pay all delivery charges.'

No problem.

'And we take six months to get it to you.'

Whatever you say.

'Give me a chance to think, I've never got this far before.'

241. **Never talk down**:

Unless you are a competitive negotiator that specifically uses tactics such as **running down your product** or **what do you know** it is better to bear in mind that you are dealing with another person, a person who wants to be respected and not treated like an idiot. See **respect** and **let them save face**.

242. **Nibbling**:

After the deal has been signed they deliver it two days later than agreed, and there are two or three of the products missing out of an agreed package of 100. Maybe it's not the colour agreed, or the exact model, but close. Nibbling, nibbling, nibbling and unless you stop them you end up with something that wasn't in the contract. "I'm afraid I ordered a chess set but instead of 32 pieces there are 29. And they're draughts. And the board is a snakes and ladders board."

243. **No air con and no water:**
It has been shown that when students are put in a hot room without water their thinking processes and their results on tests are lower. In a negotiation a well hydrated negotiator has an advantage over a dehydrated one. Be especially careful if you are going from rainy Manchester to negotiate in Abu Dhabi.

244. **Non-negotiable/un-discussable**:
This tactic is seen regularly walking hand in hand with **Stonewalls** and **Commitment ploys**. When the agenda is first marked out you get certain issues taken off because you automatically say they cannot be discussed. Take note of these and remember them later when you are in the exchange stage. Sometimes if offered the right incentive later on in the negotiation, previously un-discussable issues suddenly become completely up for debate.

245. **Not Losing What you have:** (see **reframing**).
It has been shown that people are two times more averse to losing something they already have than they are motivated by the prospect of getting something new. This means that you should emphasise, where possible, how much money they will save, how they can protect investments already made, and keep themselves and their family safe and disease free!   Then go on to mention the

added features and the "Snow globe with real glitter" they get for signing the contract.

246. **Nothing agreed until everything is agreed:**
This is a standard and very useful line in a negotiation (unless you are a clever negotiator that likes to close issues off item by item, winning a little on each one). This is combined with negotiating as part of a package and makes sure that you can go back and reopen earlier issues if necessary to accommodate concessions on later issues. To be used with **Waterbed it!**

247. **Now or never:**   see **ultimatum** and **deadlines** and **scarcity.**

O

249. **Objective standards:**

Seek out objective standards (that support your point of view) to argue your case. No matter how passionate you are, no matter how persuasive you are, you will do a lot better if you are armed with facts, figures and reports that were not generated by your company. Any time spent digging this information up will be more than rewarded when you can shoot their **low/high balls** out of the sky and back up your arguments with solid unbiased standards (house prices for a certain region, standard car prices for given models etc.)

250. **Off-the record:**

In a negotiation nothing is off the record. It might not be written down while you are saying it but it will be recorded (in an elaborate negotiation you might be recorded without your knowledge.) and brought up later if it suits the other side to do so. However when you use the expression "this is purely off the record"   you can make an offer sound more genuine, and you can also get the other side to open up, "in the spirit of the moment".

251. One good turn deserves another:

See **reciprocity.** Reminds them of their obligations. Also follows **gift giving**. However you may also preface a concession with this to show you are A) making a concession B) honouring debts C) cancelling debts D) continuing a virtuous circle.

252. "Only 40 cents a day!":

Dividing things down into their individual units can be an effective way of making the overall deal seem more appetizing. In modern marketing televisions only cost 2 dollars a day – for the rest of your natural life, or if you pay 100 euro a week you can pay off that car in time to give it to your grandchildren, each grain of rice only costs 1 cent (what a bargain!) etc.

253. Open door:

As simple as the label says – leave the door open in the meeting room (even better if it's behind them). They can't relax or ask you for favours as anyone can be listening and on top of it they have a draught on their back which will have them shifting in their seat after no time.

254. **Open on a positive note:**

Start with 'well, we are all looking to do a deal here today" or "We're sure looking forward to doing business with you" or anything else, no matter how insincere, to start the negotiation off on the right track. If you start as you mean to go on it will make the rest of the negotiation easier.

255. **Or else:**

See **threats**. Instead of hurting the other side overtly these 'or else's could be making them aware of their losses if they don't reach a deal: "...or else you could continue to lose money every day." "...or else you could stay with your current supplier and pay twice the amount we're offering you." "...or else you could wait until next week and hope that we haven't gone somewhere else with your business." In this second set of 'or else's the tag line "it's your choice" is added regularly.

256. **Outnumbering**:

Having more people on your team than on theirs can have many advantages and a few disadvantages: you can intimidate the other side; you can **Tag Team**; you can assign different people different roles which they can specialise in; there are greater opportunities for finding solutions etc. The downside is the potential for **Divide and Conquer**, people contradicting each other, costs of so many on the team and coordination.

257. **Overt intimidation**:   See **Big Body, Yelling, Personal Insults, Threats**

258. **Overwhelm**:

This works in two ways: You can ask them for so much information that their system breaks down – thus undermining their authority, they waste time on digging up information, or they could become defensive instead of offensive. The other way is using the **power of confusion** against them where you overwhelm them with too much information and then offering them an **"it's that easy"** solution.

P

---

259. **Package**:

Always try to put a package together. If you have only one issue to present to the other side then you are stuck in **Haggler's Universe** until you meet somewhere in the middle (or closer to the person with the bigger gun). When you negotiate as a package you can **Waterbed** it or **Add and Subtract** and you could benefit from **increasing the issues**.

260. **Padding**:

This almost always happens in a negotiation though the degree changes from person to person and from country to country. Padding is increasing your prices/costs to give you wiggle room when you are negotiating.   If the other side accept the initial prices you have proposed all the better. If they don't then you can make concessions down to your real price.

261. **Paid Up Front:**

Get paid up front. This is related to the concept of the declining value of services. After you have performed a task that people badly wanted (going to the dentist for example) those same people have fuzzy memories and can rarely remember how much they wanted the service beforehand. Get your money before you pull the tooth.

262. **Pity** – see **go easy on me**.

263. **Paper Crown:**

Pretending you have authority when you have none. There are many occasions where people will not negotiate with you if they feel that you do not have the authority to take a decision. Pretending that you do in fact have that authority is what the Paper Crown is all about. They go all the way to the end of the negotiation with you believing that you have the power to close. It is only then that you make a call to the home office to confirm everything or pass it onto the next level. The other negotiator will not be happy and it's not great for building trust but as far as you're concerned you have done your part.

264. **Patience:**

.... is a virtue. There is a now famous experiment that was carried out with small children many years ago. They were given a sweet and told that they could eat it immediately, or else they could wait a while and be given two. The children were re-interviewed years later and it was found that the children who were able to wait for the second sweet (those who were able to delay gratification) were happier and more successful. In a negotiation impatience almost always hurts you. An ability to wait, stay calm under a dragging timeline, and sit there waiting for your two sweets is not so much a trick as a skill you should develop.

265. **People like you:**

An example would be when selling to lawyers you say: "80% of lawyers in your field in this city use this perfume." **People like you** plays on two influencing factors: first we believe that if people who are like us do or use something and are happy with it then we will probably like it too, and second the need to conform to the habits of the group that we belong to. Of course if you can identify the most visible and trend setting people in each group and convince them first it will be easier for you to convince the rest. When this tactic is applied to you perhaps you should ask yourself "Is it pure chance that the other lawyers in my field use the same perfume. Will I be a better lawyer if I use this perfume? Will anyone smell that perfume and say 'There goes one hell of a lawyer.'?"

266. **Perry Mason Ploy:**

Get the other party to say 'Yes' repeatedly until they get into a momentum and will then say 'Yes' to things that they may have said 'maybe' to before. Do you like red? Yes?

And do you like cars? Yes? And do you like fast cars? Yes.
And would you like to buy this fast car today? Yes.

267. **Persist and don't desist:**

Are you like a dog with a bone? A negotiation can be a
long, drawn out process and if you have the ability to
persist with it you are not only showing that you are really
interested in doing business with the other side, you may
also wear them down so they give in on a particular issue.
(This is not the same as hounding a customer into
submission, which is another tactic altogether (**coercion,
hustle close**)).

268. **Personal Insults:**

Used in the following case or cases: if you are specifically
brought in as a bad cop; if you are never going to negotiate
with the other side again; if you have all the power and you
don't care about the long term consequences; or if there is
no chance that they will go completely ballistic and shoot
you or walk out on the negotiation. You would need one or
all of those situations and a personality that has no
problems insulting another human being.

You can do this to intimidate the other side, to make them
feel that they, and by extension their services/products, are
worthless, to make them angry (see **anger provoking**) or to
get them to leave so that you can negotiate with someone
else (more amenable) in their company.

269. **Perspective taking**

Negotiating is about seeing the deal through your opponent's eyes, not your own. That doesn't mean thinking 'what would I do in their shoes?' It means 'what would <u>they</u> do in their shoes?'

270. **Phasing**:

Don't try to do everything at once. Within the stages of the negotiation you can always sub divide down into phases. "We are going to look at issues ABC in this round and in the next round we are going to look at issues DEF." You can also phase the implementation of parts of the agreement as well before advancing further with the agreement. Phasing is especially useful when it is a conflict negotiation and there are specific issues that can derail the whole negotiation and impede progress with any other areas.

271. **Physical intimidation**:

This can take different forms. It could be something as simple as **Big Body,** to invading their personal space as if you were doing it unintentionally (this is a common misunderstanding between people from different cultures and one side often ends up feeling uncomfortable with the close proximity to the other side – or their cold distance!). It could also be the fact that you feel your health/life is threatened because of the people you are negotiating with, the person who is standing at the door behind you or third parties waiting for you outside. Even though you may be in a situation where logically you know that the other person cannot kill you, the very fact that you have a very big person leaning across a table shouting in your face can speak directly to the Neanderthal inside us all and we will feel intimidated. Then all the negative elements of **Fear** enter your negotiating game.

272. **Planted information:**

This means leaving information where they can find it. It might be taking a break for coffee and leaving that information on the table. It might be throwing it in the waste basket where you have your private team meetings. It could be forgetting it when you leave the room and then coming back later to retrieve it ("oh, clumsy me!")

This should be used convincingly and with people who have no ethical dilemma about looking through your documents when left unattended.

In that planted information you can give a false impression as to your strengths or the fact that your management has indicated there is no way you can budge on certain issues. You might even leave genuine information behind so that they are sure you are not bluffing.

Be careful with assuming afterwards that the other side has definitely read the information you have planted and working on that basis. There are honest people in the world after all, you just might be lucky enough to be negotiating with them.

273. **Playing a broken record:**

Coming back to the same issue again, and again, and again. Not letting the other side off the hook when they don't answer the question you have asked. Repeating a request even though you were given a 'no' initially. Stating your position and saying it again like a mantra every time they try to get you to make a concession. It can be very frustrating to deal with someone who does this, and some people may even make the mistake of giving them what they want just to stop them playing that broken record! With a response like that even just some of the time it is no surprise that they continue doing it.

274. **Playing dumb:**

The important thing in a negotiation is not to look dumb *after* the negotiation. However if looking dumb in the negotiation helps you then forget about your ego and do it. Asking the other side to repeat themselves, checking with experts to confirm information, spending time to understand exactly what you have been presented with, asking for clarification, apologising for making a mistake because you didn't understand clearly what you were replying to. By acting dumb (or having no problems with not being Einstein) you may also make the other side feel over confident (confidence is good, overconfidence is not) and sloppy.

275. **Poker face:**

Some people seem to be born with an impassive expression that gives little away to indicate how they are feeling. This might not be a great face for making friends but it can be excellent in a negotiation, particularly in the bargaining part of the process. Try to be aware of your own body language. Do you go red up to the tips of your ears when you are under pressure? Do your eyes twinkle happily when you have just been given something unexpectedly good? Do you start rubbing at your nose when you are nervous? Practice different possible scenarios with a friend while working at keeping your face immobile until your body remembers that lack of emotion in a real negotiation.

276. **Positive end note:**

Even if there were insults and pies being thrown in the negotiation you should always endeavour to end on a positive note. This does not involve hugs and kisses. It may simply be acknowledgment that you 'agree to disagree' before parting ways. The important thing to remember is that you may be doing business with these people in other contexts at other times, or simply to remember that you are creating a reputation for yourself, and that shouldn't be a reputation for being a sulky child that slams doors .

277. **Post-op:**

Looking at the negotiation after you have finished to see what you could have done better, and what you did well. Whether this is part of a string of negotiations with the same people or a once off there is always something you can learn and bring to your next negotiation. Doing a post-op is essential when you have been negotiating as part of a team that negotiates regularly together. Each negotiation is a process and negotiating in general is a *learning* process.

278. **Power of Confusion:**

If you use information overload on the other side (on the surface in order to help them take a more informed decision) then their capacity to calculate and decide is actually impaired. They may then go with the status quo (which may suit you) as the safest option, or even look to you for guidance on what they should do (Bingo! They are in your pocket). Some shops seem designed to confuse you so that you have to ask a shop assistant for help, and once you do that there is a greater chance that you will buy.

279. **Power of Only:**

It's only one word but it's a powerful one. This only costs $10,000 (well, if it's *only* $10,000 then I'll buy that apple). We are *only* going to decrease the amount by 100 a month. This is *only* for a limited period of 2 months and then we will be back to normal. This product is the *only* one on the market with these features. We are *only* offering this product to you. You are the *only* person who is going to get this discount. It can make something seem small (price or quantities) or special (you, product.)

As far as you are concerned, if this is being done to you, then try to play back everything they have said without 'only' and see how it sounds to you now.

280. **Precedents**:

Try and find any precedent to support your case (no matter how tenuous it is!). When asking for something it is always much easier to do so, and defend your position, if you can say that it has already been done that way/to that degree sometime before or somewhere else. It is then up to them to argue the validity of your precedent or accept it and then they are at least **anchored** by your precedent even if they decide not to give it to you exactly as you asked for it.

281. **Prepare!**

This is not a tactic, this is a strategy. You should adopt the attitude that for every cent spent on preparation you will save or make ten cents in the negotiation (or ten thousand). Going into a negotiation having thought about what you are going to negotiate, the context, the people negotiating and possible solutions should be standard for you.

282. **Prioritize:**

Of course you should have already prioritized your own interests but by asking the other side to put in order of importance what they are asking for you are doing two things: 1) finding out what is really important to them so you can focus on those issues and 2) communicating to them that they are not going to get everything they are looking for, thus lowering expectations and paving the way for bargaining.

283. **Priming**

You can put people in a certain mood, or frame of mind, by 'priming' them before the negotiation. Evidence shows that if you have images of money, or even briefcases in a room then people become more selfish and worried about themselves – a good moment to sell them life insurance. The same arguments were used against references to money when selling something like diamonds – generally a gift for someone else.

We are humans, and we are strongly influenced by context, more than we like to admit. If you are already thinking in a certain way, or about a specific thing, or feeling a specific emotion, then your brain can follow that groove in one direction or another when it comes to the negotiation itself. This is why so much time can be spent creating rapport, building trust, controlling the place of the negotiation etc. as people are aware that this can have as much influence on the outcome of the negotiation as the arguments used in the main body of the negotiation. (See **Labelling**)

284. **Problem solving questions**:

You can focus on the problems, you can focus on past conflicts, you can focus on differences, you can look for someone to blame, OR you can ask problem solving questions. 'So how are we going to stop this happening in future?' 'So how can we solve this?' 'What can we do from our side to make sure your needs are met?' This takes the focus away from recrimination and puts the emphasis on the issues to be resolved.

285. **Process not result:**

A negotiation is a process, not a result. Try to impose a process on the negotiation so that each step is followed carefully. This makes it less likely that you will make mistakes, ensures that it is easier to prepare and also enables a smooth handover if someone else has to step in and take over the reins of the negotiation (on either side).

286. **Props:**

Bringing documents, working samples etc. in a show and tell spirit can be the key to winning the other side around to your arguments. People are generally more visual than auditory and another large group is kinaesthetic – they like to touch things. If you bring props with you to the negotiation and bring things clearly from the theoretical realm to reality, you gain an advantage over your virtual competitors.

287. **Proximity:**

When there is not a serious imbalance of power or a serious clash of personalities then physical proximity can help overcome apparent conflicts. The very act of being in the same room and seeing the other person as another human being encourages greater co-operation and a desire to find a solution. It has also been shown that when people cannot see who they are negotiating with they are more competitive and use more selfish tactics. So if you feel this is the case then do your best to make sure that you can negotiate face to face.

288. **Punish Power:** See **coercion**

This also refers to your ability not just to force them by putting them under pressure, but can also involve withdrawing your support, existing deals, offers etc. Coercive punish power with a child would be smacking them, while punish power would be not talking to them. If you are part of that school then you know how effective in the short term this power can be at bending the child to your will. In the long run you the risk of having no trust, closeness or relationship with the same child and they leave home and never look back. The same may happen with your counterpart in a negotiation if you use Punish Power regularly.

289. **Puppy dog:**

Try negotiating with someone with huge eyes and the most innocent expression on their face. They almost come across as childlike. They ask you for help in understanding difficult contracts. They are effusive in their thanks when you help them. They have just arrived in the big city from the country. They may describe everything as 'super'. Now try and kick that person. Most people can't, even metaphorically speaking.

Just like it is not socially acceptable to take candy from a child there is a part of many people that screams 'No' when you are given the opportunity to bring all your power to bear and slam the other side when the other side is like a puppy dog. It's very difficult to justify your actions with 'well, they would do the same to me if the shoe was on the other foot' when the other side clearly wouldn't. As a general rule, this seems like a very fair and laudable action, unless your counterpart is only acting the role of a puppy dog and they are actually a Doberman in disguise. As a genuine strategy it works well, as a hidden Doberman strategy it can be doubly effective.

290. **Puppy dog close:**

This is a standard close. "Why don't you take it home with you for a week and see if you like it. If you bring it back we'll refund you the full amount." Try taking that puppy away from your kids after a week. Not so easy is it? The same happens when you have been driving a car around for a week, using a particular model of smartphone that you couldn't survive without after a week etc. etc. Possession creates bonds which are difficult to break.

Q

---

291. **Question tags**:

Question tags are effective ways of getting people to agree, aren't they?   And then when they get into a habit of agreeing with you it's easier to lead them in the direction you want, isn't it? You should try them, shouldn't you? They sound insecure, don't they?   But you find yourself agreeing with the speaker, don't you?

292. **Quivering quill:**

Very mean and very effective. People are ready in the heart of a negotiation to push and pull and fight tooth and nail over every single point.   Then when they feel the negotiation has finished they relax and they stop fighting. Then, when the other side is about to sign they hesitate.

'I'm not sure. 5% seems like a lot.'

'Alright, listen, let's just leave it at 3%'

'Oh, all right.'

You have just given away 2% that you had spent two hours stubbornly refusing to budge on in the middle of the negotiation.

293. **Quid pro quo:**

I scratch your back, you scratch mine. Even the very expression quid pro quo reminds the other side that they have to follow through on their obligation to return what you have given them 'We were hoping for a bit of quid pro quo.' The evil and common answer is 'Well, we never asked you to give us that.'

R

---

294. **Rags**:

Dressing poor and acting poor to convince the other side that you have no money in your bank account. This is to accompany **Empty Pockets**. Of course this may not be a trick and they genuinely are broke. The beauty is that it is very difficult to know if they are telling the truth or not. However if you are not artificially inflating your price it shouldn't matter if they are or not, the price is the price.

295. **Reciprocation**:

I scratch your back and you scratch mine. The problem with reciprocation (which studies say is something that goes back to the very basis of civilization in all cultures) is that very often what you give in return has much greater value than what you received. More often than not what you received in the first place was something you didn't even ask for – meals, drinks, free hotels, a brown envelope stuffed with cash, a concession on an unimportant issue.

Without you realising however you find yourself giving back something that you had never planned on giving.

296. **Red herring**:

You lead them on a wild goose chase. Get them to focus on areas that are not important, get them to spend time, energy and resources arguing those cases or looking them up or defending them. If the negotiation is time dependent from their side it is a good way to put them under pressure. It is also a good way to get them to NOT look at other areas that are important to you, or where you are weaker.

297. **Reducing choice:**

Give a limited number of choices to people. Not only is this so that you can control those choices, and therefore the result, but also so that you can avoid confusing the other side (which could lead them to not going with anything you offer and sticking to their present, nice and simple, supplier)

298. **References to how unimportant this deal is to you:**

See **disinterest** and **reluctant seller/buyer.** Again it is important to remember that you should be careful of giving the image that you do not need this deal, but not that you actively don't want the deal. If you are too convincing about not wanting the deal then they might just walk away (especially true in literal cultures). You should only say you do not want the deal at all when you plan to come back to it later in a **by-the-way** or grudging fashion. Also there are cultures where it is expected of you to say you don't want the deal even though everyone involved knows that you do.

299. **Referencing a benchmark:**

It is hard to argue with objective standards, even if it is an unofficial benchmark (X company charges Y amount). It is much easier to argue your case if you can reference a benchmark. This links to **legitimate power, objective standards** and **precedents.**

300. **Reframe**:

If perception influences what is being negotiated then changing the way people look at the deal can often lead to unexpected solutions. You can be very obvious about it and start with "Let me put it another way" or else you can present something as an entirely new proposal and see if they bite. You might say:

'We are asking for people to work at the weekends. We want people to come forward of their own free will. We will pay double time for these hours in compensation for the free time you are losing out on."

Or instead you could try:

"We will pay double time for hours worked at the weekend to those who choose to do so but not everyone can avail of this opportunity as we can't pay everyone so much money. We will be operating this on a first come, first serve basis"

Same thing, reframed, different impression. One argument works with one type of person, the other works with another.

301. **Rehearse**:

If you are an inexperienced negotiator, or not very confident, then rehearsing is an excellent tactic. Practice things like saying "no" and then shutting up. Practice being offered incredible wonders and not letting your eyes light up. Practice steady breathing while a friend insults you/shouts at/threatens you. If you rehearse like this there is a greatly increased probability of you acting the same way in the negotiation. Muscle memory means your auto pilot takes over under pressure, but because you have rehearsed the right response you will let yourself down less often.

302. **Relationship**:

See **friendship** for the mild version. The extreme version is 'Come on, I'm your cousin, cut me some slack here.'

303. **Reluctant seller/ buyer**:

This is a given. Never look desperate. See **disinterest, references to how unimportant the deal is** and avoiding the **Winner's frown**. Negotiators can smell your *Eau de la desperación* cologne. Few of the unscrupulous ones will not take advantage of it if they sense it.

"Oh, you absolutely need this deal for the survival of your company and we are the only suppliers of the piece you need? Of course we'll reach a fair deal.'

304. **Rephrased negative**:

With a rephrased negative you never actually commit to saying one thing, rather you commit to what it's not. Instead of saying something is good you say "It's not bad". The important nuance here is that later you can quite truthfully say 'I never said it was good" when they try to quote you out of context, or if you want to backtrack on something you insinuated in the negotiation. If you are dealing with someone who uses rephrased negatives all the time you may have to pin them down with sentences like "are you saying it's good?", "Does that mean you think it's good?"

305. **Reputation**:

Also see **Big Reputation**. Guard it with your life and be wary of ruining it for short term gain.

306. **Respect**

This is another cheap concession (**Let them save face** and **never talk down**). No one likes to be treated like an idiot (unless they are **Playing Dumb**). Unless you are specifically adopting a competitive strategy which makes the other side feel bad be careful of disrespecting the other side. This sounds obvious but you should ask yourself at different stages throughout the negotiation if there is anything you are doing which may be causing offense to the other side. Particularly important when doing business in another culture (especially ones where Personal Honour is highly valued). It doesn't mean you are soft on the issues. It means you do not add irritators to the equation by accident.

307. **Rest**:
Even if you like negotiating it can be stressful, draining and physically tiring. Plan for breaks, plan to disconnect, plan to rest. Sometimes going to a hotel in their home town is better than negotiating with them in your office after a night of getting up every hour to change nappies and feed babies. (**fatigue** and **consult with pillow**)

308. **Reward in heaven:**
"You might not make as much on this deal as you could but God will look well on you when judgment day comes." If you are a nun/doctor/social worker you have a better chance of this approach working for you. See **Appeal to your better nature.**

309. **Rollercoaster:**
Nice one minute, nasty the next. By taking them on a rollercoaster of emotions they don't know where they

stand with you (and yet ironically they appreciate the Dr. Jekyll ten times more after having seen your Mr. Hyde). This uncertainty leads them to be grateful for when you are in nice form and return concessions for concessions in the sincere hope that you don't go nasty again. Unless your personality leans this way naturally this can be a very difficult manoeuvre to carry out. A psychologically easier version for you would be to do a variant of **Good Cop, Bad cop** with someone else who is happy to be the Nasty Cop. It also means that there is less risk to the relationship the main negotiator has developed with their counterpart.

310. **Rosy future:**

You paint a wonderful picture of the future. However you paint that in broad strokes and you don't give the details. If they do ask about the details and you are good at bluffing then you can muddy the waters with "Don't worry, they'll all sort themselves out, everything will be fine on the night."

311. **RRP is recommended:**

RRP stands for recommended retail price. Recommended. Not fixed. Recommended. Never take the list price or catalogue price as a given. Ask for discounts, or "under what circumstances could you come down on that?" or "if I buy two how much would you give them to me for? And two dozen?" Some people hate negotiating and specifically use list prices to protect themselves. They prefer no deal to the stress of haggling with you. Fine, you have to respect that but that's no reason to accept it as a default setting.

312. **Rub smooth.**

This tactic may be especially useful for conflict negotiations. Through time spent together (even better if isolated in a Camp David setting) the two sides begin to see each other as human and treat each other differently. Through close proximity they rub the corners off each other and the negotiating relationship becomes smoother. Lots of hard-line organisations specifically avoid being put in these situations to avoid any reduction in their dehumanisation of the opposition.

313. **Running down your product and your service:**

Why they would want to possibly buy what you're selling after they have spent the entire meeting knocking it into the ground is a mystery unless they might be cynically trying to lower your expectations, show disinterest, try to intimidate you into accepting a lower rice or simply confuse the hell out of you and make you uncertain and nervous in the negotiation. Maybe that's it. Just maybe. Watch out for them combining this with **'what would you know?'** and **rollercoaster**.

314. **Russian front:**

Giving two choices, both bad, but one worse. Stems from the German commanders trick in World War II of getting their soldiers to carry out unpleasant tasks or else be shipped off to the Russian front. "We could give you this car at 5,000, no warranty, only 500,000 miles or this other car at 15,000, no warranty and 600,000 miles. You'll have to choose one as we don't have any other left in stock." If you are standing in the only rental company at the airport in a small country then you have been presented with a Russian front. Any **or else** or **threats** are aggressive forms of the Russian front (and similar to the original one). A very mild version is **Comparing**.

S

---

315. **Salami (slicing)**:

Slicing little bits off the deal, slice by slice until you have eaten the salami. Every tiny slice adds up to a whole sausage so be careful of being salamied. They add one percent on here, get you to pay the insurance, increase the payment terms by two days, etc. and all of this turns into a very bad package for you. Individually (if you negotiate item by item instead of as a package) you don't notice each little slice being pared off. This is **nibbling** before the deal is even signed.

316. **Scarcity**:

If something is easy to get, both in quantity and time availability, it loses allure (and value). Something which is (even apparently) more difficult to get and only available for a certain amount of time increases in value. This is the power of January sales, luxury cars and an artificially reduced supply of diamonds. You can even make your time scarce and not be up for a meeting at the time they initially offer. Hence the fact that so many people with empty agendas, pause on the phone for a moment and say "Let me check my diary and I'll see if I'm free" before agreeing to a meeting.

317. **Scout**:

Do your homework on the other side, where the negotiation is going to take place etc. Don't be caught out on the day because you didn't go at least an hour before to see the meeting room or simply do some goggling on the internet to see if there is anything on it about the person (not the organisation, that's a given) that you will be negotiating with.

318. **"See you in court!"**:

Threaten legal action, as simple as that. Negotiation over, lawyer up and ship out. Walk slowly away from the meeting room in order to give them a chance to call you back and reconsider. See **Threats**.

319. **Self-interest**:

The best way to get someone to do something is to appeal to their self-interest. The only person who (might) do something for you even if it hurts them to do so is your mother. Let's suppose for the moment that you are not reading this book to help you negotiate better with your mother. Identify what they want, identify what makes them happy, what motivates them and see how you can use that to your advantage.

320. **Sell cheap, get famous**: see **fame**

321. **Separate people from the problem:**

Depending on whether you are a competitive or a principled person you will read this statement in two different ways: If you are competitive you will understand this to mean – treat the person as unimportant, just as long as you get what you want. If you are principled you will understand that you should treat them both as equally important, but separate, and just because you are nice to them, and want to build the relationship it doesn't mean you will make concessions.

322. **Sex:**

See the **honey trap** and add "extreme", see **reciprocity** and understand favours in the widest sense, see **blackmail** and think of your spouse finding out, see **friendship** and think of friends with benefits. Be very suspicious in the middle of any ongoing negotiation if you find yourself in bed, smoking a post-coital cigarette with a young, beautiful person from the other side or even from your own side for that matter.

Another use of sex in negotiations is the refusal "to give it". Showing just how affective and ancient this tactic is, you only have to look at Aristophanes' satire 'Lysistrata'. In that play the women of Athens and Sparta are fed up of the war between their two cities. They refuse to make love to their husbands until peace is made between the two cities. Spoiler alert: it works. It doesn't take a huge stretch of the imagination to see how that might be used in the 21st Century.

323. **Shock opening:**

See **high ball** and **low ball**. This can also be good for breaking their expectations at the beginning of the negotiation and extreme **anchoring**. Sometimes it also used to make a subsequent request seem even more reasonable than it actually is.

324. **Silence is golden:**

The first side to speak after a period of silence is the side that makes the concession. Be comfortable with silence, don't try to fill it. It can give you time to think and reflect, and in many western societies it puts great pressure on the other side. Practice in front of a mirror if you can't with a friend – make an offer and then shut up.

325. **Silence – prolonged:**

Taking the silence is golden concept to its extreme means not answering them even when they do make an offer. If they are very nervous and have been bluffing until then you might find that they negotiate against themselves in a desperate bid to fill the gap. There are famous examples of the Japanese (who normally pause before answering) not getting an opportunity to speak as over eager traders talk themselves down instead of waiting for the Japanese to start speaking again.

326. **Silver line it:**

You can point out the negative side of something in your proposal. Doing this will make you appear more open and trustworthy. Then you turn it into a positive which makes the second message more persuasive as you appear to be giving both sides to the argument.

The danger of course is that the negative message will also stay in their head. This can, however, be useful when you know they will discover the negative on their own and then may wonder what else is being held back. By bringing it up first you already have the positive argument prepared and linked to the problem as a solution.

> 'Sure it's slower than other models, no denying that, but it is a tank and you can just drive over other cars in the parking lot to get to the space closest to the door.'

327. **Simple solutions:**

"Fifty-fifty", "you pay the price and we look after everything else" (**zero extras**), "you take the car on odd days and I'll take it on even days of the month", 'let's flip a coin' etc. etc. Simple solutions might not be completely fair if you examine them in detail, and if you pushed you could probably haggle more out of the other side but the lazy part of you just says "fine, let's go with that" and you accept the simple solution.   Try and see if you can think of any simple solutions (that suit your side) that can be used to break an impasse at the end (or even better if you can suggest them at the beginning and finish the negotiation straight away.) See **"it's that easy."**

328. **Sizzle**:

This comes from the expression, 'sell the sizzle, not the steak'. See also **appeal to their heart.** Find out what's cool, attractive, and intangible and sell that, not just the product. Also see **Differentiate or Die**.

329. **Skimmers**:

Those nasty little people who get in at the end of the deal and approach you to ask for their cut of the deal – or else they will scupper it.   They may be officials or relatives or local hard men. What initially seemed to be a good deal has now come with a 10% discount.   Of course, if these skimmers are working with the people you have just been negotiating with you have been doubly conned.   This may be a tactic if deliberately employed by the people you are negotiating with.   You sign, thinking you've negotiated a great deal and then find out it's not so good when the skimmers come calling (having being tipped off by your counterparts that the deal is concluded).   In another world the other side might have to pay these people off from their profits. In this world you do.

330. **Sky's the limit:**

High expectations. Whatever you think you are worth, add a little/lot. The idea as far as streetwise negotiators are concerned is that if you get what you are asking for you will definitely do better than what you had initially planned. If you don't then you will still get what you had originally planned for. Happy days both ways.

This is **high balling** and **padding** in psychological terms. Be careful of going too far – though you would be surprized how far that can be. Most people know the weaknesses of their own offer better than the other side and tend to downplay their expectations.

331. **Small seats and tall tables:**

This is using the location against the victim, ahem, negotiating counterpart. If you are totally merciless then giving them the lower seat so that you are looking down at them (especially when put in front of a tall table so they feel like they are six years old again), seats with uneven legs so they concentrate on keeping their balance etc. No matter how little mental energy they spend thinking about their discomfort a competitive negotiator is happy as it is less thinking time they have for the negotiation at hand.

332. **Smile a mile**:

If they are smiling they are more likely to agree with you. Unless they are actual evil torturers they will find it difficult to hurt you while smiling. The Flamingo style would have this has one of their central tenets. They believe that by using tricks and tactics such as 'I have two children too', 'fake smiles', 'hospitality', 'friendship' and 'flattery' they charm you so that you make concessions while feeling good about it. On the basis that the aim of the negotiation is for both sides to be satisfied, not for the pie to be split evenly in two, then emotional satisfaction and happiness can also be taken into the equation.

333. **Softener**:

'I'm afraid', 'unfortunately' and similar phrases to introduce a difficult point instead of coming straight in with the body blow. These verbal softeners are designed to take the personal out of the attack/criticism.

334. **"Sorry, you were saying...."**:

They take phone calls, speak to other people, let other people enter the office and deal with them - all while you are trying to speak to them about the issues on the table. This may be because they run their office like a multi-tasking octopus (and there are cultures that accept this as normal) but the effect can be to make you and your offer feel unimportant.   That will lower your expectations, and that, my friend is reason enough for competitive negotiators to use this tactic deliberately.

335. **Sorry**:

It has been shown that people who apologise for small things (like arriving late or knocking something to the ground) create greater rapport with the other side at the beginning of a negotiation or meeting. Apologising sincerely in the middle of a conflict situation can completely change the whole atmosphere of a negotiation. A simple 'Sorry, you are completely right, we shouldn't have done X' at the right moment can diffuse an angry situation and show that you are genuinely interested in the other side, and in finding a solution. Again, do your homework on the culture where you will be negotiating as there are countries that will take this a weakness.

336. **Spies**:

Sounds terrible, doesn't it. Yet they are used – all the time. If you ask a friend to keep an eye on your boyfriend/girlfriend who works in the same office building you are employing a spy, however you dress it up. In a negotiation for high stakes, getting the services of professionals (or being part of an organisation that has a unit of them) pays huge dividends (setting aside all ethical dilemmas this may cause you). You gain information about their next moves, about how real their alternatives are, what their levels of power are, and of course as much juicy information as you can to **Blackmail** them. See **Listening devices.**

337. **Split the difference:**

This looks fair. Let me repeat that again – 'this *looks* fair.' Whoever has said the price/value/position second decides where that mid-point is. You may think that it's fair but try to remember who set that mid-point. The second thing to be careful of is if they get *you* to offer to split the difference. If you make the offer then they may accept the mid-point you have offered as your new position and still stick to their own. If you split the difference again then you will discover that it is now much closer to their position that it is to your original position.

Example: You start at 10 and they start at 30. You offer to split the difference and they stay where they are but argue that you are obviously willing to move to 20. You continue haggling and then you offer to split the difference again. Now you are at 25. Not so fair.

338. **Squashed at a table:**

If you give the other side a table for four, and there are six on their team, then watch while they elbow each other, fill each other's personal space and get in each other's way. They spend more time pushing each other than concentrating on the issues at hand.

339. **Stakeholders:**

Go and speak to your counterparts' stakeholders and get pressure put on them from fifth columns within their own organisation to accept your deal (depending on how you do this you might win the battle and lose the war if you gain the long term enmity of the other side. If you are involved in a takeover struggle that will remove the management that you are negotiating with then this becomes a moot point). These stakeholders may include trade unions, suppliers, family members, shareholders etc.

340. **Stalemates**: see **deadlocks**

341. **Stalling for concessions**: see **delaying tactics**.

342. **Stamina**:

This is the ability to stick to your guns and keep pushing on a certain point and not buckling at the first sight of opposition, and it also refers to the physical ability to continue negotiating for longer than the other side, less affected by **fatigue, hunger** or **alcohol** as the case might be. A serious advantage in protracted, intense negotiations. It is sometime worth putting a negotiator on your team due to their stamina and not necessarily their ability.

343. **Standard terms:**

Even if they are not standard, if you present a set of terms as such   for your company, this industry, this type of operation then people will very often go along with them. Bring a copy with blanks for names as if it is indeed a standard contract. Unless they ask you to rip it up and start from scratch you are at an advantage even if they want to make changes. Because any changes they make will be on a template that you have presented them with.

344. **Status:**

Use authority, **big qualifications** and the fact that you are the boss/ duke/ sheikh/ ambassador so that **fear** and **covert intimidation** make the other side feel their offer is too high and they should reduce it, or at least they should not come out with any excessive demands that might anger the higher status person.

345. **Stonewalls:**

Not budging.   Stonewalls are combinations of and examples of **Commitment ploys, Final offer, Always say No, Non-negotiable, Company Policy, Standard terms** etc. There is almost always a way round these stonewalls if the other side wants the deal enough. You just have to find something more important to them than the stonewall (after having first tested the stonewall to make sure it isn't made of plywood).

346. Straw man:

Building something up to give it away later in the negotiation. This way the other side feels they have haggled you down and you avoid the **Winner's Frown** while also getting something of value for yourself. Many negotiations spend their time building up and knocking down Straw Men without actually trading anything of real value. Also see **Major sacrifice**, **Decoy** and **Padding**.

347. Stretch the pancake too thin to eat:

If you don't want the negotiation to work (or are trying to buy time) you can increase the issues to a number that is just too complex to be negotiated. As soon as you reach partial agreement on one area another issue appears that has to be dealt with. If this is done with you by accident then you may have to go with **decreasing issues** or **phasing**. However if you suspect that it has been done on purpose then find out as quickly as possible what the motives might be – **delaying ploy** to increase their power or simply trying to improve their BATNA in another negotiation. When you find out take appropriate steps (neuter their power or finish the negotiation)

348. Success stories: see **Big Experience**

349. Sudden changes of behaviour: see **Rollercoaster**

350. **Summarise**:

An effective and fair tactic. Especially useful if this is a conflict negotiation and you want to remind people of progress made in order to keep positive forward momentum. However it also helps to avoid misunderstandings and deal with problem issues in the moment rather than let them surface at the end and derail the negotiation. This also means that if you suspect the other side of being capable of deliberately misleading you, you are in a position to throw in their face the fact that they agreed to every summary at each point in the negotiation.

351. **Sunk cost:**

When you are negotiating you will find that money and time are spent on the negotiating process itself. At any given point in the negotiating the money/resources/time spent can be considered as sunk costs. You will never get them back, regardless of the result of the negotiation itself.

This should not influence a negotiation but it does. The longer a negotiation goes on, the more time and effort and resources that have been expended on it, the greater the commitment both sides feel to getting a deal. In theory you should write off these sunk costs as already lost (and they certainly don't improve a bad deal in the future). The reality is that people want to feel 'it was all worth it'. That means accepting a sub-optimal deal, or even accepting a deal that is clearly worse than their alternative simply to justify these sunk costs. If you need the deal more than the other side sometimes a cleverly executed strategy of dragging out their sunk costs will give you a better chance of reaching a deal. However, you always run the risk of an intelligent counterpart writing off all sunk costs to date with a nonchalant shrug and turning to their alternative. Be careful of transaction costs growing to a point where the deal does not make sense.

352. Supersize me! See **Add-ons** and **Brooklyn Optician**

353. Surprize:

Sometimes coming out with something (verbal or non-verbal) that surprizes the other side (not simply restricted to a shock opening and not necessarily negative) you can break down carefully constructed poker faces and see what they are really thinking about something. It might involve you being disarmingly honest or giving them everything they have asked for and more (if you see their eyes light up you know you are going in the right direction). Later you can retract everything as stating that you were only 'what if-ing'. If you have done a particularly effective job of your surprise you may have left them disconcerted for a length of time afterwards as they are left reeling. If you are going for an air of unpredictability and you are not very worried about the relationship this may a useful trick in your bag.

354. **Sweeten this deal:**
Backload all the problems and costs so that what they are paying the week after the deal is done is small compared to what they will be paying in a few years from now. If you are negotiating with managers instead of owners this may be an effective tactic. They may be more worried about the short term and looking good than they are about the long term health of the company (someone else's problem). By sweetening the deal you often can get everything you want, if you are just a little bit patient. If you put this together with **funny money** you can work financial miracles for your side.

T

---

355. Tag team:

When you negotiate as part of a team then you can keep up constant pressure on the other side by taking turns to negotiate. This can be effective if you are negotiating against just one person and a decision has to be taken at the end of the meeting. When there is one person they have to respond constantly, thinking of questions and answering them with little time left over to analyse long term benefits/costs of unexpected proposals. When you are part of a tag team you can sit back and size up the other side while they are being asked questions, and pick up on subtle signals that you mightn't if you were playing a more direct role in the conversation. And of course there is the added benefit of not becoming mentally exhausted.

356. Take it or leave it:

This is one of the more typical negotiation lines, and very risky, unless you have a serious imbalance of power and it is in your favour, or else you are convinced the other side are bluffing and you have already been negotiating for an age with them (or your alternative to this negotiation is great and you want to avoid pushing up your transactions costs here by beating around the bush). This line demonstrates that you are not prepared to make any (more) concessions and this is the best you have to offer.   It also indicates that you are not going to spend any more time on the issue. However if you start off the negotiation with this line it comes across as inflexible, extremely direct and unwilling to spend any time discussing the issues with your counterpart.

357. **Take notes:**

Do not rely on your memory (and be delighted if the person you are dealing with does). Take notes as you are negotiating (even better if you have someone assigned that role) so that you can quote back to the other side exactly what they said earlier in the case that they have contradicted themselves (if you do this from memory they will simply say you got it wrong). It is also good for summarising at different stages of the negotiation. And at the end of the negotiation you are in a stronger position to offer to draw up the contract on the basis of the notes that you have been taking. Many people will become more cautious about what they are saying if they feel that you are taking notes so if you feel that they are opening up and telling you things 'off the record' you might want to make a symbolic gesture of putting your pen down. Also at the very beginning of the negotiation when you are trying to create rapport with the other side you may not want to be seen to be recording everything they are saying. Other people who might otherwise be offensive as an intimidating tactic may want you not to take notes as they don't want their abuse to be recorded. However, they may even tone down their attacks if you dutifully take down what they are saying. You will probably be assailed with "Will you stop writing down everything I say!" To which you can reply "I just want to make sure I can remember everything perfectly afterwards, was that 'son of a' or 'some of a'?"

358. **Taking a break:**

This is especially important if you are negotiating as part of a team. You will need to take a break to discuss what you have heard and plan your next steps, away from the negotiating table and the ears of the other side. If you are negotiating as an individual it can be a good idea to take a break to assimilate what you have heard and get your energy levels (mental and physical) back up to speed for a fresh round. To this extent negotiation is just like boxing and it helps to sit down and rest for a minute before going back into the ring. Of course, if you are tag teaming you can prevent the other side from getting that break.

359. **Tapered concessions:**

It is important not to be erratic in your concessions or you will confuse the other side about where you are willing to settle and as a result you may never reach a satisfactory deal. One of the techniques for correct signalling is to taper your offers. This means that every successive concession is smaller than the previous one so they can see more or less where you are willing to stop. You can start with a concession of $100 dollars and then $50 and then $25. You will only confuse the other side if you go $50 then $100 then $15.

360. **Tears**: see **crocodile tears.**

361. **Tech smart:**

If you have a technological advantage over the other side (this can range from understanding technology to actually having tech resources) you can use this to your advantage in several ways: spying, getting real-time information, communicating with your home office more effectively, confusing the other side with terminology they don't understand (confusion power), impressing the other side (and appearing to know more than you do), offering to help the other side with their technology deficiencies by sharing (**reciprocity** and opportunities for **spying** on whatever they use your devices for)

362. **Test assumptions:**

This is not a tactic; this should simply come naturally to you in the negotiation. Do not assume that the beliefs you held before the negotiation are true. Make a point of checking them to see if they stand up when you make contact with the enemy. Do not even make the assumption that what they are telling you is true or is necessarily false. Be ready to be surprized if you discover that your assumptions are wrong. To make assumptions is normal, and we all do it, to hold on to them out of laziness is not acceptable in a negotiation setting.

363. **Testimonials**: see **Big Experience**

364. **Thank you:**

The negotiation is rarely a once off, and even if it is, it pays to get a good reputation out there. Don't forget to thank people afterwards, even better to send a note, and depending on the culture, an appropriate present.

365. **"That might be the case where you come from but...."**: see **culture**, that's the way we do things here. This acknowledges their point and makes it difficult to argue with yours. You aren't saying they are wrong and you are right. You are saying you are both right and different.

366. **That's not what your boss said:**

This can be an unfair line or not, depending on the context. First you could be trapping your counterpart on the back of a vague idea that their manager said to you in another context. Now however you are putting forward that vague idea as a statement of fact. Or else you could be lying to see the reaction of the person in front of you (and see whether your money was on the button and they can make a concession, pay a higher price etc.).

On the other hand you could be genuine and insisting on consistency. If you were promised or told something by their superior it is better to get it straight out there rather than wasting a day haggling back to that original position. Let them consult with their manager if they want. If they come back and say that what the manager had said earlier doesn't stand then you should go through everything else the manager said immediately to avoid any other nasty surprizes later   .

367. **The long walk:**

Making it difficult for them to get out of the building without some kind of a deal. This could be something as dramatic as the media waiting outside to hear news of the deal (with all the negative consequences of publicly saying no deal was reached) or someone with a gun waiting outside ready to shoot you if you don't sign the paper (hopefully less common). Or else it could be something as simple as being in an industrial estate in the middle of nowhere, knowing that you are going to have to take a lift back into the city centre with the person you are negotiating with.

368. **The model on sale is sold out but we have this other one....:**

A classic vendor's tactic. You enter for the incredible offer in the brochure or on the window and discover that it is out of stock. They then push the next best model on you. They can also do this when they have set up the meeting with you and they are in your office. Designed to get the foot in the door. Works enough for it to continue being employed.

369. **The more you.... the more you:**

"The more you think about 'Product A' the more you will want to buy it". By creating links between issues you can create false causal relationships that will influence the other side. The more you use this product the more you will thank me in future. The more you think about this proposal the more you will realise it is the right fit for your company.

370. **The Organisation:**

By referencing vague groups as the reason you are insisting on something, asking for something, or to explain why something is being done, you are making it difficult for the other side to pin down that group and argue with them. If you tell your counterpart that your manager doesn't agree then they might want to speak directly to your manager. If you reference the organisation/senior managers/board of directors/your parliament then it will be difficult for them to force you to call them all together to change their minds.

371. **The perfect solution/magic wand**:

Find out what their interests are by saying 'imagine I had a magic wand and I could give you everything you wanted - what would that look like?' You are not promising to give them anything but you might get a better chance of uncovering what all their needs and wants are. If you are lucky and they respond favourably to this invitation your next step is to get them to put them in order of importance. See **prioritize**.

372. **The truth:**

When there is a complete lack of trust between two parties then opening up about your true intentions or something that has happened internally can disarm the other side and work towards creating trust between both sides ('To be honest we were hoping for a bigger discount on this product as it was part of our plans to expand into the southern region next year.') The surprize factor alone can shock the other side out of the current dynamics.

373. **There is more than one way to skin a cat:**

Go into the negotiation with options. Remember that in a negotiation it is unusual for the other side to accept your first proposal. Don't be surprized therefore when you have to change your initial offer. It is better if you go in from the beginning with different ways to satisfy your wants and needs to avoid haggling from positions or stonewalling yourself into a corner.

374. **Third party experts:**

When you bring people in from outside they lend an air of objectivity to your arguments which makes it more probable that they will be accepted by the other side. These experts can range from officially independent parties such as mediators to experts on a specific subject that can attest to the reliability of the figures and information you are putting forward. If the other side does this, test how much of an 'expert' the expert actually is and don't be afraid of bringing your own experts to argue your case. Most of the time there are two sides to every coin and you will find people who are able to defend any argument (if they are paid enough).

375. **Threaten:**

This is a staple of any competitive negotiator's arsenal. "We'll fire you/we'll go on strike/we'll kill your family if you don't give us what you want." There are people who are happy to make threats and people who aren't. The question here is whether they are effective or not. If the threat is credible then the other side may feel they have no choice but to accept your conditions. Not only that, but a threat is generally something that creates **fear** in the other side. When people are frightened they spend less time on thinking of positives and more time spent on the negatives that you are expounding. Fear also has a restricting effect on people's thought processes, turning usually intelligent individuals into the mental equivalent of sheep. However if the threat is tested and it proves to be false there will be a backlash of anger which could ruin any chances of a deal for you. Also if you use threats you will find that the other side arms itself to make sure you cannot threaten them again and will look for other partners to do business with at the first opportunity. Be careful of using threats but the fact that that they are constantly employed attests to their (ruthless) effectiveness.

376. **Tick tock:**

Using time against the other side. Especially useful if there is an event happening in the future which the other person cannot control (return flight, the end of the reporting year etc.). Time is power, and the more you have of it the more power you have. See deadlines and false deadlines. See **Deadlines, False Deadlines, Time Pressure Cooker.**

377. **Time Pressure Cooker:**

Use urgent language (body and verbal) to put them under pressure. Hurrying them, looking at your watch etc. If you can infect them with your sense of urgency you can get them to overlook elements of the contract (hustle close) or to make concessions before you leave. This is fine if they are desperate and you have all the power. Otherwise they may break the negotiation due to irritation or because they crack under the **Time Pressure**.

378. **Tit-for-tat:**

Some say this is the most common (and effective) type of negotiation. "I will co-operate as long as you do. As soon as you punish me or treat me badly then I will reciprocate." This way, if both sides play ball a positive relationship can develop and both sides benefit. Using this strategy also discourages the other side from behaving badly. In negotiation simulations the problem arises in the last round when there is no chance for revenge – in theory both sides are encouraged to use competitive tactics. This bears out in the real world where once off negotiations encourage these kinds of tactics also.

379. **Town crier:**

Telling the media. This can be an effective way of trying out new ideas, shaming the other side over tactics used at the negotiating table, getting proposals taken off the table that wouldn't be advantageous to your counterparts stakeholders (trade unions, shareholders etc.), signalling acceptance of potential proposals put forward in the media by the other side (see Trial Balloons). Using the media has its price however as they can also end up scuppering the deal if information is leaked that can ruin the whole affair.

380. **Training, spare parts, etc.:**

Add extras to the table to increase value and to avoid being reduced to negotiating over price. You may be selling them a product but in today's world that very often means that you can also propose to sell them training, warranties, after-sales service etc. Always examine your proposal to see if you can differentiate from your competitors. See **increase issues**.

381. **Trial balloon:**

You are not sure if something will be acceptable to the other side and you don't want to lose face by proposing it. You can get a third party to suggest that proposal and then see how your counterparts react to it. If they react positively then you can formally propose it and take it from there. If they react badly then no-one has been embarrassed and the proposal is never officially put forward.

382. **Trust:**

Once you have gained the trust of the other side you can get away with murder. Once you have lost their trust you have an uphill battle ahead of you. To establish trust think about the people involved, the history that has gone before and what measures you could use to establish credibility and trust with them. Perhaps you can gain trust by being open, making goodwill gestures, choosing a neutral venue? By not abusing your power. By showing you are consistent. Little by little you should demonstrate that you a man/woman/child of your word. Gaining people's trust is important. Unfortunately this can be used for ill as well, but not having any trust makes ethical requests and bargaining more difficult also.

383. **Try and fail:**

This belongs to the Toucan negotiator's arsenal. By telling people to "try and find a problem with the package", "try and find a better offer with the competition" it automatically implies failure (hypnotists use the same psychology when they tell you to "try and resist" as the very word 'try' implies that you won't succeed). At a subconscious level people here the failure of the word 'try' and react accordingly – i.e. they give up.

384. **Turn things upside down:**

Creativity is a tactic that should be encouraged. Spend time with your counterpart or with your own side trying to come up with non-obvious solutions that would benefit both sides. Spending a little bit of time on exploring unusual possibilities might be the key to getting past stalemates and haggling. See **Brainstorm**.

385. **Turning Tigers into Vegetarians:**

This is the opposite of a trick; this is something you should not do. Believing that you can get an aggressive negotiator to stop attacking you by making concessions is the same as believing that by giving enough meat to a tiger you will turn it into a vegetarian. Do not reward aggressive tactics because you are only encouraging them. The key here is **conditional concessions.**

386. **Two translators:**

You can use a third party to translate for you and then watch and observe your counterpart's body language as they speak to the interpreter. If you understand what they are saying then you can also use the time when the interpreter is translating to think of a suitable answer. On the other hand your counterpart has to respond immediately to the interpreter and then wait while this is being translated into a language they do not understand.

U

387. **Ultimatum**:

See **take it or leave it, or else, deadlines**. The type of ultimatum can change from what you are offering, to how long you are offering it for, to the type of threat you are issuing them with. The danger of an ultimatum is that it damages the relationship if they accept it and it destroys the negotiation if they don't (or else your credibility if you were bluffing). However there are times where you have grown frustrated with the negotiation's progress, with the constant haggling over minor details and the feeling that they are simply using **delaying tactics** on you, for whatever reason. If your BATNA is something that can be measured in money terms and your time can also be measured in money terms then you may calculate very quickly if it is worthwhile issuing an Ultimatum to move things on or switch to your next best alternative away from this negotiation.

388. Uncover

...Everything. Your objective in the negotiation (if it is anything more than a simple haggle in a street market) should be to try and uncover as much information about the other side (weaknesses, motives etc.) as possible. This is not preparing (also essential in a complex negotiation) – it is in the negotiation itself. It means designing a proper questioning policy and creating the right atmosphere for getting answers.

389. Understand perception:

What we think we see is not necessarily reality. This very basic concept is often forgotten when you are negotiating and yet it is what negotiations are all about. You perceive the same thing as having a different value to the way your counterpart sees it, hence the negotiation can progress. Changing perception and understanding how it can affect you are essential to negotiating well.

390. Understand power:

If you do not understand the balance of the power, or naïvely think that power has nothing to do with a negotiation then you are at a serious disadvantage in this negotiation. There are many different types of power, from personal (charisma, experience, reputation) to resource (money, time, people, force, information) to situational (third party support, legitimate, BATNA). You should do an analysis of the power in the negotiation at the beginning as part of your preparation and then periodically reassess the situation throughout the negotiation to see if the balance has changed.

391. **Understand role of media:**
See **Town Crier, leaks, trial balloons**.

392. **Understanding value differentiation:**
What is important is knowing what it is worth to the other side, not what it is worth to you.   This is the basis of negotiating.

393. **Unique:**
If your product, service or idea is unique, truly unique then it has its own value. It's not that it necessarily does a better job than other similar offerings (**Differentiate or Die**) but that it is the only one of its kind.   Another useful tool to counter objective standards and price negotiations. People are more inclined to want something that is rare and unique.   Something which serves no practical purpose but is the only one left in existence makes its value shoot up. Is there anything Unique about your service, product or proposal that you can point out?

V

---

394. **Vague language:**

It is useful at the beginning of a negotiation to not be too clear in definitions used. This ambiguity permits both sides to interpret the initial statements the way they want when they are selling them to their own side. Later however as the negotiation progresses this kind of vague language can actually create problems as the implementation becomes messy due to the different interpretations.

395. **Vague modals:**

You *may* find this, you *might* find that. By using vague modals (may, might, could) it is easier to present statements that can be accepted or argued with, without any serious loss of face for the people proposing. If you make a definitive statement with antagonistic people you are inviting them to find exceptions to it. When you use vague modals you are saying that your proposal is possible and general but not necessarily applicable all of the time or with all people. This can sound more reasonable. Later your vague modals disappear when you have moved further on in the negotiation. 'You may feel that the best choice is 10% down and the rest to be paid in 90 days' changes to 'So, we're going to go with the 10% down, rest in 90 days option.'

396. **Visualisation**:

If you visualise something before you do it then it becomes easier to do when the actual moment arrives. If you have used visualisation techniques effectively your body 'remembers' having done it and does it again in real life. Athletes, sales people and public speakers do this often to motivate themselves and to prepare before an 'event.' It has also been shown that if a salesperson can get you to see yourself using a product or service then it will be easier to convince you to buy it. 'Just imagine yourself, driving down the M30 in this car, windows rolled down, your favourite music playing, not a care in the world.'

W

397. Walk away point:

Fallback position: Redline. Know the point beyond which you will not go. This is a must in a negotiation. If you don't know what your lowest limit is you may bargain hard and well and still end up with a worse deal than no deal. For many competitive negotiators, especially in the exchange stage of the negotiation, it is all about finding out what the other side's redline is and pushing them as close as possible to it.

398. Walk out:

If you feel that the negotiation is going nowhere, if you have a better offer, if you want to fake indignation, if you want to push the other side into accepting your offer because you're not staying for anything less, if you feel that the other side aren't taking you seriously, if you feel that by staying you would be going against your values – then fine, walk out. It can be very effective. So effective that some drama queens walk out several times in the same negotiation. What you should not do is storm out because you are really angry and you haven't thought through your actions. Walking out and slamming the door sometimes means that you have to crawl back in later when you realise your mistake.

399. **Wants and needs:**

Sometime you have to explain, patiently, to the other side the difference between wants and needs. "We understand that you *want* X,Y and Z.' However, we feel that what we all *need* here is A,B and C.' It can be a good idea to show them that their request is unreasonable and they are potentially sacrificing a potential deal out of a childish desire to get what they want. ("I want that toy!")

400. **War**:

The ultimate threat. This can go from real war to media war to strikes to calling your mother-in-law. Use war carefully, consciously and sparingly. Threatening war shouldn't be like crying wolf. Say it when you mean it, because if you are bluffing you will lose all credibility in the negotiation. And if you do threaten it make sure you are aware of all its consequences, to everyone. Do you have what it takes to see it through to the bitter end?

401. **Waterbed it:**

When you sit on one side of a waterbed it goes down and the other side goes up. The shape changes but the size remains the same. When you are negotiating it is always useful to negotiate as part of a package. That way they can press down on one part of the package but that means that somewhere else it's going to go up for them. This can be very useful as you can keep pushing in different parts of the package until you find a shape that suits everyone – without reducing the package.

402. "We should have been told":

This is part of the post-official stage of negotiations. A good example is when a house is being built. The builders discover extra difficulties that weren't in the original plan and make the necessary changes and add-ons as they are building. They then try to charge you for these essential extras. You refuse. 'I'm sorry, but we should have been told if you were going to deviate from the original plan. We're not paying for that.'

403. "We've never done that before":

If they have the balance of power in the negotiation they can insist on something simply because they are not prepared to do something new, potentially risky or just down right innovative. This can be especially frustrating if you are trying to find a creative solution to a problem that will suit everyone. If you are dealing with people who do not like change then you will have to think about how to rephrase your proposal so that it is presented as a continuation of whatever they are already doing as opposed to something radically different. Otherwise come back with "what if....."

404. **We're all friends here....:**

These are the words they are using. What they might be saying is: Do not read the contract carefully; Accept the small increase I have added on or you will look mean; I will do you a favour in future; I am being magnanimous about this tiny concession because this deal is like the cat getting the cream, in a diamond bowl, for my side; I am saying we are friends because we aren't but I want to create a false sense of camaraderie to get you on my side.

On the other hand if the situation has gotten out of hand and tempers are rising, it can be a good idea to use this phrase to remind people of the importance of the relationship and to call on all parties to try and resolve their differences.

405. **We can change that later:**

Used when referring to mistakes in the contract. . It very often comes from people who use **friendship** in the negotiation to get what they want as well. Unless there is a long term relationship of trust between both parties (and even if there is) insist on the necessary changes being made before you sign anything. It is very difficult to get those modifications made after the contract has been signed.

406. **What do you know?**

Undermine their authority. This is said in a condescending voice and you can do it about anything that people know but can't prove, unless they are an absolute expert.   .

This is a direct form of intimidation. You can make the other side angry and defensive, or you can make them doubt themselves and feel uncomfortable about presenting ideas in future in case you shoot them down. This can be an aggressive tactic to use against the opposition but on your own team it stifles creativity and motivation (and yet everyone knows someone who speaks like this)

407. **What if?**

"What if" is a good way to put proposals on the table when a deadlock has happened.   It is even a good way to introduce the proposal stage of a negotiation.

'Let's just imagine. No threat here, we're just using our imagination. I know you have said your position. And it's a good one. Just for a moment though let's go crazy. What if you didn't ask for a ten per cent increase and simply accepted the price as it is?'

408. **Why not?**

Don't accept a simple 'no' or refusal. Explore for more information. Find out what is motivating them. Find out what the consequences are of them doing something. Maybe you will be able to relax them about the options you are presenting them with, maybe you will simply understand their point of view so you don't offer something else that doesn't suit them, and sometimes they may even realise there is absolutely no reason why they shouldn't do something (some people automatically say no, and others say no because what you are proposing didn't work in the past or in another scenario – but would here and now)

409. **Widows and orphans:**

When negotiating do not say 'If you give us this deal then the big farmers in my country will become so wealthy on state subsidies that they will all be pulling their ploughs with Ferraris.' Instead you should say 'If you don't give us this deal the small farmers in my country will die early. Think of the widows and orphans they will leave behind. For the love of God have mercy. If you're not going to do it because it's right for you then do it for the children.'

410. **Winner's frown:**

The trick is in avoiding this. You get exactly what you wanted but you feel it was too easy and therefore you are not happy with what you achieved. Set yourself clear goals for the negotiation and if you reach them break out the champagne, do a thorough **post-op** and learn for the next time.

411. **Withdraw offer:**

By withdrawing an earlier offer (especially after a deadline) you are putting them under pressure to accept any further offers without haggling. Sometimes, if they are desperate and you know it, they will make concessions just to get back the earlier deal you had offered. You can only use this tactic if you are in a position of power, really do have a better offer somewhere else, or feel that unless they are put under a modicum of pressure they will never hurry up and close the deal.

412. **Wolf in sheep's clothing:**

Pretending to be a soft negotiator, a soft touch, and easy to push around, you should be careful about assuming that your counterpart is as dumb/innocent/soft/weak as they are making themselves out to be (of course they might be). Are you buying a car at a bargain (thinking you are taking advantage of them) that turns out to be a lemon? Are you pushing them around and getting more arrogant by the moment and then you are trapped by your ego? Are you sure that they don't have a clue so you don't check the figures that they are presenting you with? Don't be the shepherd that gets eaten.

413. **Writing the contract:**

Sounds like extra work? Yes, it is. A little bit of extra work with huge rewards. You decide what goes into the contract and then you let the other people pick it apart – working from the contract that they have written. You can write it with nuances that support your side but say more or less what was agreed in the negotiations. If you are totally unscrupulous you can add on some percentages that just aren't worth starting the negotiation over again to try and resolve. You can leave things out and hope the other side won't notice.

414. **WYSIWIG:**

What you see is what you get. See **Zero Extras.** Transparency combined with '**it's that easy**'. If you have nothing to hide and no padding added then this can be a point of differentiation right on its own.

X

---

415. **X-ray:**

Make everything apparently transparent. You show them exactly what you are going to charge for every single item (broken down), preferably doing a **9.99** on it, so that they feel every figure has been justified. You then say that you cannot go down any lower as you are clearly on cost in every single area (or else you can do a **major sacrifice** on a few small issues, leaving the rest alone). The beauty of an X-ray is that it looks more official and because you are being so transparent it looks as if you can't go any further on any issue. The downside is because you have been so transparent they know exactly what you are charging for each individual item/service and therefore they can haggle with you on every single point and compare more easily with competitors.

416. **Xtra Mile:**

Go that little bit further than you had offered or promised. Like a **last concession lost** but after the deal. This builds trust and increases goodwill for future rounds of the negotiation. Done from a position of strength, not weakness.

Y

---

417. **Yelling and screaming:**

Some people believe (rightly on occasion) that if they kick up enough of a fuss they will get what they want. You will see them in hotel receptions shouting at the receptionist that they want an upgrade because their room is disgraceful. You might have a boss who is like this and makes life hell for you (the people who stay put up with it, those who can't leave, while the boss unfortunately stays the same). In a negotiation it can make the whole process very difficult when you are dealing with someone like this. You might be tempted to simply give in to get them to shut up, or change negotiators so they become someone else's problem.

418. **You'll have to do better than that....:**

They do better or they run the risk of stalemating the negotiation. Very often the answer to this is simply 'well, perhaps we could give you a 5% discount on...' This is a very simple haggling line. There is nothing unethical about it because it contains no explicit threat, no coercion, no lies and no manipulation.   It is as simple, and effective as the package says.   It is just one line that said at the right moments can improve an offer, for nothing in return.

419. **Your competition......:**

One of the oldest tricks in the book. Starting a sentence with: '*(insert name of company)* offers five percent more on that particular model.' 'Jim from XXXX was in here the other day and he offered me the Thingamajig 4.0 for half the price.' Etc. What do you do? Pray to the Small Gods of Speechless Negotiators that your product has differentiating features which makes a direct comparison impossible. You can always come back with 'You can't compare apples and oranges.' You will have a slightly more difficult time if they come back with ' I'm afraid you both sell oranges.'

420. **Your friend John already drives one:**

This plays on the influencing factors of social proof, liking and 'keeping up with the Jones'. Sometimes by saying that 10,000 people in another country eat a particular type of cornflakes you can persuade someone to buy that brand of cornflakes. However it can be even better to tell them that 100 people in their own company eat that brand of cornflakes and better still to say that 10 people in their neighbourhood eat those particular golden flakes of corn.

421. You've got to be kidding me/ you can't be serious:

Belittling the other side's offer. By showing that you are incredulous you are making them reappraise their offer immediately. It is a softer version of 'Are you stupid, there's no way we're going to accept that.' Gives the same message without the insult. Should be accompanied by shaking of head and sharp exhalation of breath (see **flinching and wincing**)

Z

---

422. **Zero extras**:

In a negotiation if you can offer someone a service or product and assure them that there are no extra costs this is an effective argument (No added VAT, no freight charges, no service charges, etc.). See **Power of Simple Solutions, WYSIWYG** and **"It's that easy!"**.

# #

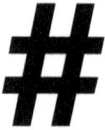

423. **30 Second Sell**

In a negotiation be prepared to have your main argument summed up in a few lines (if you were selling this would be called your 30 second sell). What is your main line of attack and your main reasons for believing that they will accept your proposition? This will help you keep on target if you are put under pressure and if you are negotiating as a part of a team it will give a general direction (commander's intent) for your colleagues.

424. **80/20**:

Remember that 80 per cent of the concessions are made in the last 20% of the negotiation so make sure that you hold out until the end with your biggest concessions or they won't take you seriously.

425. **"9.99 it"**.

It has been proven that numbers that are not rounded sound better in a negotiation (9.99 vs 10.00, 7.86 vs 8.00 etc.). The potential client feels that the price has been carefully calculated. Therefore they feel that it is the correct price as opposed to a random price that has been picked from thin air. To gain the full effect it should be a number close to but below the rounded figure (.99 instead of 1.03)

426. **9/10s of the law**:

There is an expression which says 'Possession is nine tenths of the law'. In a negotiation this is easy to understand. You have sold your products to the customer. They have received them. You haven't been paid. Now that they have the products it is a lot more difficult for you to get your money from them, or the products back. Think of a rented flat where the tenants are not paying you and you can't get rid of them. It can be so difficult in many countries to get them out that you finally accept the fact that they leave after a few months without paying their back rent rather than spending a year in the courts trying to evict them (without the certainty of getting your money back, or finding the flat wrecked when you do get it.). In a negotiation you don't simply have to negotiate a good price for your products/services, you also have to think about how you are going to get paid in the negotiation instead of fighting it out in court afterwards that you are owed the money. Think ahead, always.

Notes

In most cases in these notes only the name of the book and the author is given as the full publishing details can be found in the Select Bibliography section. Where articles are quoted, their full information is given here.

1. **The Eagle** Negotiating style follows the Principled or collaborative style closely and is heavily influenced by the work of Roger Fisher and William Ury, starting with their seminal work *Getting to Yes*. The five original elements of their primer on principled negotiation are: focus on interests, not positions, use objective standards for legitimacy, separate the people from the problem, creative solutions for mutual gain, and power through a strong BATNA.

2. **Acceptance speech**: The idea of writing your opponent's victory speech comes from William Ury's book *Getting Past No*.

3. **Acknowledge:** One of the important elements in principled negotiating is to separate the people from the problem. Rather than pretending that people do not exist, it actually means that they are treated as a separate problem to be dealt with. It is identified that people have strong emotions that can upend and derail

a negotiation and that it is important to take these emotions into account. In their book, *Building Agreement*, Daniel Shapiro and William Ury discuss the important role that emotions play in a negotiation, and strategies for dealing with them. One of those is to acknowledge the other person, which does not mean agreeing.

4. **Always say No**: The experiment with holding back the toys so that they become more valuable to the child (a dramatic increase in demand for a toy that is more difficult to get than a toy which is easy to get) is detailed in Robert Cialdini's book *Influence*, under the section on Scarcity.

5. **Apparent choice**: 'if you can get the bird to walk into the cage on its own, it will sing that much more prettily.' Robert Greene, *48 Rules of power*, Pg 259.

6. **Appeal to your heart:** As Jim Camp states in *Start With No*, decisions are 100% emotional. The idea is that we take our decisions with our heart and then justify with our head.

7. **BATNA baby!** To the best of our knowledge BATNA has become a common place word in negotiation literature but the first to use the term were Fisher and Ury in *'Getting to Yes.'*

8. **Because:** The earliest example of how effective this can be was carried out involving an experiment with queues

for a a photocopying machine where simply inserting the word "because" in the sentence 'Please can I use the copying machine because I want to make some copies' allowed over 90% of the petitioners to jump the queue. For the full experiment read Langer, E, A. Blank and B. Chanowitz (1978), *'the mindlessness of ostensibly thoughtful action: the role of 'placebic' information in interpersonal interaction'.* Journal of Personality and social psychology, 36: 639-42.

9. **Big Experience**: Robert Cialdini, *Influence*, discusses the tremendous power of Social Proof, demonstrating just how strongly we are influenced by the fact that other people have already done or bought what we are being asked to do/buy.

10. **Big heading:** While there are many experiments which show the power of confidence in convincing and persuading people I like the one described by Victoria Woolaston which talks about how bloggers who 'shout' louder and are more opinionated are considered more trustworthy by their readers than bloggers who look at both sides of an argument. See *The best way to win an argument?* Victoria Woollaston 30 May 2013 dailymail.co.uk. For further examples see Dutton's *Flipnosis*, pgs 239-244.

11. **Body language**: The percentages on the power of body language are convenient misrepresentations of an experiment carried out by Mehrabian in the 1970s but the message is equally valid – body language can

often be a greater source of information about the other side's intentions than the exact words they are uttering.. (Albert Mehrabian, www.kaaj.com/psych, retrieved 29 May 2009)

12. **Brooklyn Optician:** We saw the first example of this in the excellent resource book *Essential Negotiation* by the streetwise negotiator Gavin Kenney.

13. **Cash Cows:** This concept comes from the Boston Consulting Group matrix for products (the other three categories in the matrix are dogs (low earner, low market growth), stars (high earners, high market growth) and question marks (low earners, high market growth). .

14. **Commitment trap**: The tendency for humans to want to be consistent, and the possibilities for trapping us through commitments and a desire to be consistent are discussed in detail by Robert Cialdini in his book, *Influence*.

15. **Commitment ploy:** Another tactic discussed in Kennedy's *Essential Negotiation* though the concept is far from unique to him.

16. **Comparing**: If you want to see this in more detail look at "How can a new superior product mean more sales of an inferior one?" Goldsetein et al, *Yes, 50 Secrets from the Science of Persuasion*, Pg 32.

17. **Cry me a river**: The link between sadness and negotiations is dealt with in the book *Yes, 50 secrets from the science of persuasion,* Goldstein et el. Pg 172-14.

18. **Email:** for more information on the research that supports the idea that virtual negotiations are better for weaker negotiators see: British Psychological Society (BPS). "*Face-to-face negotiations favor the powerful.*" ScienceDaily. ScienceDaily, 9 April 2013. <www.sciencedaily.com/releases/2013/04/1304092118 57.htm>.

19. **Expert**: Going back to the Milgram experiments and our weakness in the face of authority figures, there have been many studies and research carried out showing how those who appear, at least, to be authority figures can persuade us. Robert Levine explores this topic in his book *Power of Persuasion.*

20. **Fair**: The desire for fairness, as exhibited by monkeys, was shown in an experiment where two monkeys were offered different rewards for the same task. When the monkey that was rewarded the worse 'treat' saw what his companion was receiving he refused to carry out the task again and in fact threw back the treat. For the full article on the experiment go to: http://www.dailymail.co.uk/news/article-2236702/*Fascinating-experiment-shows-monkeys-bananas-unequal-pay.*html

21. **Fatigue**: The link between bad decisions and tiredness is well documented. For one example you can go to *Yes, 50 secrets from the science of persuasion* by Goldstein et al. Pg 178-180

22. **Feel, felt, found formula:** There are many authors on the subject of this formula and how it can be used to defuse arguments from potential buyers by referencing the experiences of other satisfied customers. However I trace the first use I'm aware of back to Roger Dawson in his wonderful book *Secrets of a Power Negotiator.*

23. **Foot in the door**: asking for small concessions and then big is examined in greater detail in Yes, 50 Secrets from the Science of Persuasion, pgs 55-58.

24. **Golden Bridge:** This idea is taken from *Getting Past No* by William Ury who in turn took it from the Chinese military strategist, Sun Tzu. The strategies and tactics of war are so regularly applicable in negotiations that one would be forgiven for thinking that one is simply a variation of the other.

25. **Help me to understand**: Jim Camp in his book *Start With No* describes the PICOS style of negotiating developed in General Motors which was invented to take advantage of suppliers by pretending to be Principled Negotiators.

26. **I have two kids too**. Similarity is another one of Robert Cialdini's factors of influence (*Influence*) where

he discusses how we are more influenced by people who we believe to be like us.

27. **Increase the size of the pie**: The story of the orange and both negotiators getting 'all' of the orange is a common one and appears in many guises throughout the literature on negotiations. To the best of my knowledge Fisher and Ury were the first to use it in their book, *Getting to Yes* as an example of how the principled negotiating style aims to deliver positive sum results in a negotiation.

28. **In-group, out group**: Humans are gregarious. We form groups by identifying things we have in common with others, and what we do not have in common with people outside the group. An extreme example of this is racism. However it has almost immediate effects when people identify others as part of their group. In his book *Flipnosis*, author Kevin Dutton describes experiments where people in random out-groups were punished by people in random in-groups.

29. **It's that easy:** is based on Zipf's Principle of Least effort- George Kingsley Zipf (1949, *Human behavior and the principle of least effort*, Addison-Wesley Press). People, like a river, will choose the path of least resistance. However, just like a river can meander for miles and miles instead of taking the harder, straighter path, so to can people end up paying for their easygoing approach.

30. **Just Say No**: If you have difficult saying No then I strongly recommend the book *The Power of a Positive No* by William Ury for more on this and how to develop this valuable ability in a negotiation.

31. **Labelling**: Very often people act according to how they have been labelled, or even how the activity has been labelled. The examples of how this works is numerous but I refer the one described by Daniel Pink in *To Sell is Human.* The studies on calling someone generous are detailed in Yes, 50 Strategies from the science of Persuasion, pg 59.

32. **Little by little:** Gradually escalating commitments is covered in Robert Levine's *The power of persuasion.*

33. **Make them work.:** Lego adopted an unsuccessful strategy with some of their product lines of reducing the amount of pieces so that people hardly had to work at all to put it together. Part of the story of their wonderful recovery and enormous growth involved ditching that strategy and returning to one where people who bought their products had to go back to doing a little bit of work again. The result in a negotiation can be equally successful – people own the solution and because they have invested part of themselves in it, they are more likely to implement the results. For Lego's success story see Brick by Brick (David C. Robertson, Crown Business: 2013, Crown Business).

34. **Not losing what you have**: Loss aversion is covered in many sources and how we prefer to hold onto the berries we have rather than maybe get the bananas on the tree across the ravine. One book that does is Goldstein et al's *Yes, 50 secrets from the science of persuasion*.

35. **People like you**: The power of social proof in influencing us is covered in the relevant section of Robert Cialdini's book *Influence*.

36. **Perry Mason Ploy**: This is another one from the book by the inimitable Gavin Kennedy, *Essential Negotiation*.

37. **Perspective taking:** The thought leader, Daniel Pink (*To sell is human*) points to experiments which show that negotiators who are asked to look at the negotiation from the perspective of their opponent were more effective than those that did not,

38. **Playing dumb:** One of Robert Greene's 48 rules of power (pg 156-160) is to appear to be less than you are. Once more, let me say that it is better to look stupid *during* the negotiation than stupid *after* the negotiation.

39. **Priming**: The experiments to show that people became more selfish after being shown images of money is covered in Roger Doley's book Brainfluence, pg 9.

40. **Reciprocation**. This is one of Cialdini's factors of influence which he describes in great detail in his

primer *'Influence, The Psychology of Persuasion.'* One of the human instincts that make civilization possible is the power of reciprocation.

41. **Respect**: one of the characteristics of effective negotiators as identified by Rackham and Carlisle is an ability to reduce irritators (Rackham and Carlisle *"The Effective Negotiator – Part 2: Planning for Negotiations,"* Journal of European Industrial Training, Vol. 2, No. 7 (1978)). Disrespecting the other side could be counted as an extreme irritator.

42. **Rollercoaster:**   This tactic has also been called by the colorful but less illustrative name of "the flaming Lamborghini" as it appears in the Daily Telegraph, *Secrets of Supermarket negotiators. Supermarkets & suppliers: Inside the price war* By Jonathan Sibun and James Hall, 27 Apr 2008.

43. **Separate people from problem**: One of the pillars of principled negotiating, as described in *Getting to Yes* by Ury and Fisher.

44. **Shock opening**: Roger Dooley gives the example of the highly successful girl scout who would knock on doors and ask for an initial donation of $30,000 and then come down to a box of cookies, which seemed like nothing in comparison (*Brainfluence,* 2012).

45. **Sky's the Limit**: The idea of High Expectations is a key element of Kennedy's *Everything is Negotiable* but you will find it in the works of most streetwise negotiators.

46. **Tigers into vegetarians:** Attributed to Heywood C. Broun. The full quote is "Appeasers believe that if you keep on throwing steaks to a tiger, the tiger will become a vegetarian."

47. **You'll have to do better than that:** Also known as a 'krunch' tactic as discussed in Chester Karrass's book *Give and Take*.

48. **9.99 it**: The research that shows how non-rounded up numbers are more persuasive is covered in the article *"Study suggests what wins in the art of negotiation"*, (QMI Agency June 01, 2013, www.TorontoSun.com)

Select Bibliography

Borg, James. *Persuasion*. 2nd Ed. Great Britain: Pearson/ Prentice Hill. 2007

Camp, Jim. *Start With No*. New York: Crown Business 2002

Cialdini, Robert B. *Influence*. New York: Collins. 2007

Dawson, Roger. *Secrets of Power Negotiating*, 2nd Ed. New Jersey: Career Press 2001

Dobelli, Rolf. *The art of thinking clearly*. New York: Harper 2013

Dooley, Roger. *Brainfluence*. New York: John Wiley & Sons 2012

Dutton, Kevin. *Flipnosis*. Great Britain: Arrow Books 2011

Fisher, Roger and Shapiro, Daniel. *Building Agreement, Using Emotions as you Negotiate*. London: Random House Business Books 2007

Fisher, Roger and Ury, William and Patton, Bruce. *Getting to Yes*, 2nd Ed. London: Penguin Books   1991

Gates, Steve. The Negotiation Book. New York: John Wiley & Sons 2012

Gitomer, Jeffrey. *Little Red Book of Sales Answers*. New Jersey Prentice Hall 2005

Goldstein, Noah J. and Martin, Steve J. and Cialdini, Robert B. *YES! 50 Secrets from the science of persuasion*. London: Profile Books 2007

Goleman, Daniel. *Emotional Intelligence* USA: Bantam Books 1996

Greene, Robert. *The 48 Laws of Power* London: Profile Books 1998

Hadnagy, Christopher. *Social Engineering.* Indianopolis: Wiley Publishing 2011

Hazeldine, Simon. *Bare Knuckle Negotiating.* Great Britain: Lean Marketing Press 2006

Kahneman, Daniel. *Thinking, Fast and Slow.* London: Penguin Books 2012

Karrass, Chester L. *The Negotiating Game.* New York: HarperCollins Publisher 1994

Karrass, Chester L. *Give and Take* New York: HarperBusiness 1995

Kennedy, Gavin. *Essential Negotiation.* London: Economist/Profile books 2004

Kennedy, Gavin. *Everything is Negotiable.* 3rd ed. London: Random House 1997

Lawson, Ken. *Successful negotiating.* London: Axis publishing 2006

Levine, Robert. The Power of Persuasion. New York: Wily. 2006.

Levinson, Jay and Smith, Mark and Wilson, Orvel. *Guerrilla Negotiating.* New York: John Wiley & Sons 1999

Lopez, Ben. *The Negotiator.* Great Britain: Sphere 2011

Lyons, Carl. *I win, you win, The Essential Guide To Principled Negotiations.* London: A & C Black 2007

Malhorta, Deepak and Bazerman, Max H. *Negotiation Genius.* New York: Bantam Dell 2008

McRaney, David. *You are not so Smart.* New York: Gotham Books 2012

Misino, Dominick J. with DeFelice, Jim. *Negotiate and Win.* USA: Mc Graw Hill 2004

Noesner, Gary. *Stalling for time.* New York: Random House 2010

O'Connor, Joseph and Seymour, John. *Introducing NLP.* London: Harper Element 2002

Pink, Daniel H. *To Sell is Human.* New York: Riverhead books. 2012

Raiffa, Howard. *The Art and Science of Negotiation.* Cambridge, Mass.: Belknap Harvard 1982

Ross, George H. *Trump Style Negotiations.* New Jersey: John Wiley & Sons 2006

Shell, G. Richard and Moussa, Mario. *The Art of Woo.* London: Penguin Books 2008

Shell, G. Richard. *Bargaining for Advantage.* New York: Penguin Books. 2006

Stark, Peter B. and Flaherty, Jane. *The Only Negotiating Guide You'll Ever Need* New York: Broadway Books 2003

Thaler and Sunstein. *Nudge.* London: Penguin Books 2009

Ury, William. *The Power of a Positive No.* New York: Bantam Dell 2007

Ury, William. *Getting Past No.* London: Century Business 1992

.